REVIEW
DIVORCE BLUEPRINT AND
JOURNAL

Vicky Townsend:
Co-Founder and CEO The National Association of Divorce Professionals

"Wow! Do I wish I had this when I was going through my divorce! I never knew about divorce coaching when I was going through it, but boy would it have made a difference in the outcome of my divorce and my life. Her advice and experience will guide you through a complicated process and will save you heartache and money and will set you up for a better future. Do yourself and your family, especially your children, a big favor and take the time to do the work in this workbook. It will be the best investment you make as you embark on this journey."

Keli Hazel, CPA, Financial Planner and Author of *Suddenly Single*

"Man oh Man do I wish I had a Better Divorce Blueprint when I was going through my divorce. Methodical and a life saver come to mind. Will definitely recommend to my clients contemplating or in the throes of divorce. A necessity to get you started on the right track personally and financially."

Barbara Bell, Founder Bell Divorce Advisors, AIF, CDFA, CDS
Certified Divorce Financial Analyst

"Better Divorce Blueprint is a must read for anyone facing divorce, no matter which phase they're in. This easy read is an outline for protecting property, rights and your heart. The author looks at each phase of divorce from a place of love and patience, to help families move through the difficult process with ease and understanding."

Samantha Lennon, Partner Heredia & Lennon Family Law LLC, Family Law Attorney

"Paulette's comprehensive guide to divorce is a must-read for anyone who is contemplating or currently going through the divorce process. As a divorce attorney, I would recommend it to all of my clients without hesitation. Better Divorce Blueprint is a game changer."

Tierra Womack: MBA and Founder of The Brave Way Confidence and Success Coach, Narcissist Abuse Expert

"This is a must read for anyone going through divorce as it blends real world advice, practical strategies and actionable exercises which leave the reader feeling empowered, believing that they too can come out better on the other side of divorce no matter what!"

Martin F Kane II : McGrath and Kane Inc., Esquire

"Anyone who is about to embark on a divorce needs to read this book prior to calling a divorce attorney! The insight that you will glean will save you thousands of dollars but as important, save you millions of emotional dollars. That the divorce attorney is not your therapist, is tremendous advice. Reading and understanding the contents of this book, will set you on the correct path.

It will allow you to avoid the inevitable pitfalls of divorce. It will give you the knowledge and power to press on through a very difficult and emotional period of your life. Things will get better. You need to take care of yourself mentally and physically during this process. Paulette gives you the path to get through what I refer to as the "emotional blender" of divorce. Following her keys to the mental, spiritual and physical betterment of yourself will allow you to wade through this process from a much healthier perspective."

Ilyssa Panitz: Editor: "5 Things You Need To Know To Survive And Thrive During and After a Divorce," Content Director for The National Association of Divorce Professionals, Divorce News Journalist

"Better Divorce Blueprint' is not only invaluable for people going through a divorce but also for the professionals that serve them.

Anything and everything you can possibly think of and encounter during a divorce is jam packed into this book.

Custody, financial, co-parenting, moving – it is all in there and I am just naming a few.

Paulette carefully takes you through each phase of "divorce" and teaches you what you need to know so you can make clear and better decisions to get the best possible outcome."

Sonia Queralt: Family Law Attorney, Co-Founder of Divorceify

"As a divorce litigator and having been divorced myself, Paulette's book is exactly the type of resource that clients need when going through the divorce process. Paulette does a wonderful job of breaking down the divorce process and delivers insights into all of the different emotions and issues that can arise when someone is going through divorce. The advice and tips that Paulette offers clients are insightful because she is a divorce professional that has also been through the divorce process herself. I cannot recommend this book enough – if you are starting the divorce process or are in the middle of it, this book will help you every step of the way. If you are a professional that works with divorcing clients – tell them to RUN and get this book NOW."

Tracy Ann Moore-Grant, Family Law Attorney and Founder Amicable Divorce Network

"Paulette is a caring and passionate divorce coach and mediator who has developed an innovative concept for helping individuals divorce better. As an experienced divorce professional, it is refreshing to see Paulette's ideas for helping parties move through the process and onto the next chapter of their life with positivity. This book is a must read for anyone facing divorce."

Winter Wheeler, Winter Wheeler Mediation & Arbitration LLC

"In Better Divorce Blueprint, Paulette Rigo tackles every aspect of divorce and lays the good, bad, and ugly on the table. Paulette makes clear that divorce is a complicated endeavor, but does so in a relatable, compassionate,

and easy to understand way. Her empathy, understanding, and genuine desire to empower the divorcing is palpable. She pursues a holistic approach to divorce and advocates for preparation of the mind and heart, not just the paperwork. Paulette sparks joy and hope in moving on, showing that there is light and passion in being whole with or without a partner. This is a must read for anyone contemplating divorce."

Rebecca White

The work I've done in Better Divorce Blueprint as well as the year that I've worked with Paulette has transformed my life. I was a recently divorced stay at home mom who hadn't worked in my tech security field for 8 years. I didn't know what the next stage of my journey could be. A mutual friend said I should talk to Paulette. She challenged me to find the answers inside me and pointed me in the right direction.

Over the course of a year, Paulette helped me take an idea and nurture it into a business. She empowers me and validates my efforts. I went from being confused and anxious to feeling completely in control of my destiny. I couldn't have done that without Paulette's special style of coaching. She takes the time to understand where her clients are and meets them there. It's been one of the best experiences of my life and, thanks to Paulette, I'm ready for the new adventure ahead!

BETTER DIVORCE BLUEPRINT

*Divorce made smoother, easier and
better for you and your family*

By Paulette Rigo

DEDICATION

This book is dedicated to my brave clients and readers seeking freedom, empowerment, healing and a better future.

TABLE OF CONTENTS

FOREWORD

Hello and Welcome to the Better Divorce Blueprint:

Divorce made easier and better for you and your family.

This book is a companion tool to the online video course that introduces you to immediate healing, discovering your dharma (purpose) and confidently creating your best life ever while navigating the long road ahead. It can be used in conjunction with the course or read as a standalone book.

First, I give you my promise that you are not alone. I am here and so are others who care about you. I believe Divorce isn't such a tragedy. A tragedy is staying in an unhappy marriage where you feel devalued or unappreciated and teaching your children the wrong things about what a healthy loving relationship looks like. I will walk you through the entire journey in a practical approach, all while addressing the emotions of the complicated, detailed "business" agreement of divorce.

I learned that divorce is not purely the end of a relationship, it's also the end of a legal binding agreement. Let's take the romance out of marriage for a moment.

If when you stood before your marriage officiant, they proclaimed to you:

Do you promise to share all financial documents and tax returns with one another?
Do you promise to treat each other as equally invested business partners?
Do you promise to include each other in all of your decision-making processes?

Do you promise to communicate in clear, truthful, considerate and respectful words?

Do you promise to openly and authentically present yourself to your partner?

Do you promise to cherish and honor each other's sacred space and privacy?

Do you promise to never use intimate details about your partner against them?

Do you promise to treat your partner with dignity and refrain from harm?

Do you promise to grow together and support each other's passions and skills?

Do you promise to never speak unkindly about your partner to your children?

Do you promise to never ridicule, gaslight, show contempt, disregard, ignore, avoid, alienate, use, triangulate, stonewall or form an alliance against your partner?

Do you get the idea? We assume love and honor is enough.

Marriage would be a different relationship…no doubt.

While taking the course will not undo the past nor change your current situation, I do know it will help you create a different future. A better future that you deserve and desire…**even if this was not your decision to end the marriage.**

You will complete this course feeling a newfound self of:

1. Patience, inner peace and non-attachment
2. Respect for self and others
3. Peace with the process
4. Clarity and truth in what you want, need and deserve
5. Forgiveness for yourself and others
6. Strength, fearlessness and confidence
7. Excitement and joy
8. Unconditional self love and self care

Let's start to create the future you deserve.

You're considering divorce...which means the moment arrived when you feel the pain of staying in your marriage is greater than your fear of change. And now you may be overwhelmed. Unsure of what to do next, or who to turn to for answers and help. Your feelings are on a roller coaster and there is no getting off.

One minute you hate your spouse and the next minute you love them. Confusion is found at every turn. You don't know what to think, how to feel or who to trust.

Stress is your new normal. One minute you are waking up with anxiety and raging fear and the next you burst out into tears and find yourself hiding in the bathroom broken down crying, trying to compose yourself.

Thoughts run the gamut and your head is swirling with questions.

How will I get through this?
Should I stay or should I go?
Is it possible to save the marriage?
Where do I find the right help?
Do I need a lawyer?
What do I do first?
How are we going to tell the children?
How do I minimize the damage to the kids?
After 20 years of marriage how can our marriage be over?
How do I overcome betrayal?
How am I going to support myself?
Where will I, and the children live?
How am I going to protect myself?
What do I do if I don't have access to our money?

For me, I felt like I was living someone else's life. Nothing fit.

I lost my purpose and felt little joy in everyday tasks. I battled extreme sadness, uncontrollable crying, racing heart rates, compulsive thoughts and self medicating with shopping, prescription medication, wine, dalliances and avoidance. I was too exhausted to care and knew something had to change.

The guilt, shame, blame, embarrassment and loss are real. The end of a marriage is never what you wanted. You fell in love, planned your life together and hoped love would be enough to get you through anything. For better for worse…right?

I remember those feelings and thoughts. I wish I had done something other than deny my feelings. I wish I found help. I wish I knew what to do. I wish I had known that I wasn't crazy. I wish I knew I wasn't alone. I kept it all inside and prayed it would all go away. For years I tried everything I could imagine to make it all better and fix it. I read every self-help book on marriage I could find and nothing worked to fix it.

It's easy to feel that way. It's easy to feel stuck, trapped, broken, confused, angry and sad.

I was stuck too! I had a lot of roadblocks and things that kept me from knowing what to do and how to do it. We all do.

I was terrified of what my "family and friends" would think of me and say about me.
I was terrified of not having any credit in my name and no money in the bank.
I was terrified of not having any professional skills or a job.
I was terrified of not knowing where I or the children would live.
I was terrified of the rejection and disregard I may experience when everyone found out I wanted a divorce.
I was terrified of the future and how the hell I was going to cope.

There is a lie that it's ok to live like this.

There is a lie that it makes you a stronger person to shut up and suffer.

There is a lie that you must stay and suffer and try to make the best of it despite so much pain, fear or abuse.

There is the societal pressure that says…it is your obligation to stay in an unhappy marriage or that you are a bad mother if you want a better life for yourself and your children.

There is a lie that tells us that we are nothing if we aren't married and have a partner.

There is a lie that tells us that if we are single, we will be alone, worthless and miserable.

And then there are all the social media images of perfect families in front of Christmas trees dressed in perfect outfits, first days of schools and wedding anniversaries.

That was 20 years ago.
I survived, but it wasn't pretty. In fact, it was as ugly as ugly gets. I learned so many lessons.

One thing I knew for sure was I couldn't go on with the way things were going. I knew I couldn't change the past, BUT I could change the future.

The old way is broken.
The old way is wrong.
The old way is outdated.
The old way is painful.
The old way is damaging. To everyone…particularly the children.

But people think this is normal. People think this is acceptable. The way it has to be. The way it has always been.

Research, support and guidance makes all the difference. Divorce is a catalyst for growth and change where you feel heard, respected and you can manage your emotions.

But don't despair …there is a brand-new day!

I believe it can be different.

Better.
Divorce can be a new start.
Freedom. A new life ahead.

You can come out the other side more confident. You will be proud of who you were, prouder of who you are and the proudest of who you will be! You will be compassionate for those you love and always keep the kid's needs a priority. You will have self-worth. You have a sense of higher purpose. You will build new exciting and satisfying relationships.

You will restore and cherish old relationships that are fulfilling and respectful.
You will thrive on your terms.
You will be focused and make better decisions.
You feel acceptance for who you are.
You know it's ok to be at the stage you are in and to live in the moment.
You will get your life back.
You will have freedom from the grief and guilt.
You will find your voice and learn to smile again.

Let's start by prioritizing your emotions.

If you are the one who is thinking of asking for a divorce, you may be feeling guilty and pained for wanting change and giving up on your vows.

If you are the one that heard from your spouse, "I am not happy, I want a divorce" you probably feel shock, betrayal, hurt, sadness or anger that your partner wants out.

Take the time to really step back and process your emotions to allow yourself the opportunity to respond with grace and self-love.

BUT how??? I want to cry or scream.

It's time to slow down.

I believe in the 5-second rule...but when it comes to divorce, I believe in 48 hours. Never feel pressured to make a decision. Know your options, do your research, get organized, determine your why, get the support you need and make better decisions.

I am not pro-divorce... I am proactive to either make your relationship work, if that's possible... or pro-active making the tough decisions to create the best possible outcome for you, your children and your spouse.

If there is any chance of saving your marriage, please take that seriously and **do all that you can to be certain your marriage can't be fixed before you proceed.**

That does not mean I give you the green light to procrastinate or pretend you are "OK." You must do all that you can to have no regrets for ending a marriage that feels unfulfilling or unsafe.

Now is the time to make an appointment with a couples or marriage counselor. It is worth the time and expense to work out these issues, because **regret is a terrible thing.**

If you already have and you both have given counseling the work it deserves, know you gave it your all.

Therapy takes both parties to authentically want to create lasting change. It takes commitment, a willingness to hear the good and the bad and the desire to listen to your spouse without being defensive or lying. There are times it takes a few different approaches or types of therapists to make progress, but there are also times therapy is simply delaying the inevitable.

My purpose in creating this course is to address all of the uncertainty and walk you through the whole process. From the very beginning of contemplation, to the healing end of finding closure to move on with the freedom to create the next chapter of your life.

My collaboration with the founders of Divorceify: Attorney's Sonia Queralt, Casey Shevin and Tali Koss allow me to take this step by step course to a profound level of expertise and insight.

We are strong, educated, experienced and wise women who are here to share our stories and insight to save you time, money, relationships and heartache.

I am glad you are here. You are not alone. You will get through this. You will be stronger, wiser, happier and ready to transform your life. You deserve better and that is what I am going to show you.

Are you ready? Let's jump right in. It's better on the other side.

INTRODUCTION

MY STORY

Why am I the right person to coach you through divorce? Let me tell you a little bit about me and my story.

I met my first husband at the tender age of 17 and we married when I was 23.

It was my impression that dating for seven years was plenty of time to know if he was "the one." It all seemed like the natural next step. I desired to be free of living with my parents and wasn't confident enough to get a place of my own after college. I didn't want to be alone. I wanted to feel safe and protected. (I'll spare you all the drama of all that) Young love felt right and real. That was all we needed.

On our 10th wedding anniversary, I was a young mother with three small children. I loved so much about my life, but I felt lost.

Everyone assumed I was blissfully happy. (Everything was great... right?).

At the age of 23, I was disinterested in the details of our finances. I wasn't involved in completing or filing our taxes, which further imbedded my disinterest and disconnect. Yet, it was a relief and a mystery at the same time.

My parents often fought about money and I did all that I could to avoid confrontation. I truly wanted just to let him take care of the finances and I would take care of everything else. I loved to decorate, entertain and fuss over the children and kept my insecurities to myself.

I became resentful, but still pretended I was fine, **but inside I was on fire**. The less connected we were as a couple, the more I slipped into a state of sadness, fear, confusion, frustration and anxiety.

I blamed myself for our failing relationship, thinking everyone else's marriage was perfect and I was the flawed one. I was uncomfortable asking questions, so I avoided it. It ate away at my soul. I reacted by shutting down and working more. I found my escape in the kid's activities and searched for connection somewhere. I began having emotional affairs. I was searching for connection and validation somewhere. It was unhealthy, but it was how I coped. I eventually became depressed, which led me to taking several medications.

My own marriage was being held together by what was an overwhelming love for our children and the obligation to stay together for the children. I didn't want to be a walkaway wife nor did I want to endure a runaway husband. I wanted a true partnership. I didn't feel like an equal partner, my marriage felt empty and we started living parallel lives.

I knew if I didn't get clear on what my future needed to be, I would continue to damage myself and everyone around me. After an enormous amount of self-study, I gathered the courage to file for divorce after 20 years of marriage. I was optimistic that we could divorce amicably and respectfully...

It took eight years to settle our divorce and the experience was exhausting and all consuming. I experienced all parts of the divorce process from litigation, to a full trial and the appellate process all the way to the state appellate court.

I became estranged from my former spouse and our children and lost friends and family along the way. Co-parenting was extremely challenging and the attorneys controlled our divorce.

There are so many things I wish I had done differently. So many things I wish I understood and managed.

I learned the hard way and I want to save you from what I went through.

I believe there is a better way. I am here to help you have a better experience. A better outcome.

I committed myself to learn everything I could about divorce to help others through what was the most devastating event in mine. There is a better way. I believe it. I know I have seen it. I have prepared it. I have created it.

I now focus on **how** the parties can create a deliberate process. There is so much to take into consideration.

This is why I created **Better Divorce Academy.**

I fused together all of the knowledge, skills, research and experience I have gained into one unique, direct, holistic, highly personalized method I call Better Divorce Blueprint.

I created Better Divorce Academy to expertly guide and support you. I am here to save you the trauma, expense, wasted time and heartache I experienced. You can do this and I will show you the way.

Yes, it can get a bit messy and unchartered at times...but you will stay on course.

Let's slowly explore what a better divorce looks like. IS THIS MAKING SENSE?

If not...hang in there...it will.

Throughout my online course and this book, there will be prompts, exercises, worksheets and many questions to ponder and answer. For those who like to work in print, Better Divorce Blueprint Work-book/Journal is available from www.betterdivorceacademy.com with all the prompts and questions. Otherwise, you can use a notebook to complete the answers.

For those who prefer to type, I strongly recommend you use the secure online journal "PENZU" p-e-n-z-u instead of a paper journal to fill in your answers. It is double password protected to give you peace of mind. It is also accessible on your phone, tablet, laptop or desktop device, giving you quick access and security.

Any time I ask a question, **you will want to have your journal handy**. Or have your online PENZU journal handy. If you are in my online course, answer the questions at the end of each video module .... OR if you prefer, simply pause the video, write the question down, journal your answer and continue when you are done. If you are reading the book, try to pause and answer as you go.

There is no right or wrong way to do this. Experiment to see which method works best for you. Be sure to consider a secure, private place to keep your divorce journal or notebook of answers. Otherwise, you can use your PENZU journal.

I am with you every step of the way. If you are taking this course or reading this book, it's because you need to be here. I am honored and humbled you chose me to help guide you through this transformation. See you in Lesson ONE!

1

THERE IS A LOT TO TAKE INTO CONSIDERATION: GO SLOW

GET CLEAR ON YOUR WHY

In order to know why you are proceeding with a divorce, it's best to take a deep look at your thought processes.

Let's break everything down and take it one step at a time.

It's important to celebrate your small victories and **learn not to overreact to nonsense and drama**.

By taking small steps, you can gain courage and step into your new identity moving forward. Before you do anything else, please **download a digital journal** if you fear your privacy will be invaded. Otherwise, a printed journal is fine. You can use the **Better Divorce Blueprint Workbook/Journal** or a plain notebook.

Many marriages have gone off the rails because one spouse has betrayed the other's privacy and read their journal. If you **do** have a place you can write your answers down and still maintain privacy, the written word is more beneficial because the act of writing accesses deeper layers of the subconscious mind. Your responses tend to be less what you think you should answer and more what is the voice of your soul. More on that later.

So here comes a question you need to contemplate deeply…

Why are you contemplating getting a divorce? I recommend you go to my website and take the **Divorce Predictor quiz** (on the home-page) … it will help you gain further clarity. But as you will learn in Lessons 1, 2 and 3, you still need to process more deeply.

 **Let's get clear. Here are key questions to spend some time on and clearly answer in your journal:**

1. Why is your marriage feeling like you are wearing shoes that don't fit?
2. What makes it uncomfortable?
3. What makes it painful?
4. What makes it difficult?
5. Are you arguing about petty things- like putting the toilet seat down? `
6. Are you ignoring each other?
7. Are you keeping secrets?
8. Are you living parallel lives?
9. Do you see eye to eye on anything?
10. Do you speak different **Love Languages?** Written by Gary Chapman (gifts, acts of service, words, quality time, touch)
11. Or are you too similar and butt heads? (birds of a feather or opposites attract)
12. It's important to have a private place you can keep your thoughts...do you have one?
13. Have you shared your feelings with anyone?
14. Do you trust anyone?
15. You can trust yourself and you can trust me. This is why you are here. Do you agree?
16. I ask that you begin to allow yourself the honor of FEE-LING your feelings. **Make a list of your current feelings you are feeling right now.**
17. Your gut is your second brain. It's much smarter than you give it credit for. How is your health, wellness, diet and sleep?
18. What are the feelings your gut is telling you?
19. What do you truly want? If you could wave a magic wand what would your future look like one year from now? Five years from now?
20. Are you or your children in any danger?

In lesson 4, you learn to take full responsibility for your emotions and your actions. Now is not the time to finger point, blame or ignore the cards you've been dealt.

If you are the one questioning your marriage OR you are the one that has been told they are thinking of divorce... **YOU WILL have emotions** attached to those thoughts.

You're going to need to write them down. Once again, if you don't have a secure place ...**consider PENZU** or a hidden note on your phone that is password protected.

Holding on to your emotions and fear can lead to high stress and illness. As a yoga teacher trainer, I know for a fact that many people **practice yoga to process emotions, trauma and fear**. If you can't trust anyone ...find a yoga class near you or take a class online.

It's important to take care of yourself. You will need stamina and a place to unwind that is healthy and safe. Do you think you could do that?

There are a few deal-breakers. We will go into detail with those in lesson 5. It's also time to examine your emotions and prepare and protect yourself. **Are you ready for the next step?**

I know you can navigate the process wisely and with grace. I will show you the way.

Lesson One
Your Thought Process

This is a very exciting time…I wish I had a course like this when I was at the very beginning of my divorce journey. It would have saved me and my family thousands of dollars, years of precious wasted time, important relationships and heartfelt pain.

The first question we need to consider at the very beginning of the journey is this….

How do you know divorce the right thing for you? Now that you are a bit clearer answering the introductory questions, keep them close and let's continue to understand why most marriages fail.

Here are the top 21 reasons couples divorce.
(not in any particular order)

1. Infidelity
2. Money
3. Lack of communication
4. Constant arguing
5. Weight gain
6. Unrealistic expectations
7. Lack of intimacy
8. Lack of equality
9. Not being prepared (50% of divorce happen between the 4-8th anniversary)
10. Abuse
11. Addiction
12. Parenting styles
13. Didn't marry for love
14. Lack of disclosure or sincerity

15. Lack of identity or self-esteem
16. Irreconcilable differences
17. Long-distance
18. Interference from parents and family
19. Jealousy and insecurity
20. Control struggles
21. Your spouse is gay

There are a few reasons divorce may be a better choice:

1. Less financial difficulties or conflicts
2. Less conflict over different spending, saving and investing styles
3. Freedom from abusive harmful relationship
4. Less harm to children
5. You get that chance to be yourself
6. You return to a sense of freedom
7. You no longer stay stuck in a relationship that doesn't feel like a good fit
8. You open the door to being with someone who is a good healthy fit
9. Old friends, new friends and self-friend
10. You become a better, less distracted parent
11. Fresh start with ex to co-parent and be friends instead of partners
12. You get to take care of you
13. You can live your own dreams if they are different from your spouses
14. Greater control of your money and your future

MONEY MONEY MONEY

The subject that we all like to avoid talking about…

Everyone you meet in life will have a **different take on how financial matters** should be handled. Some people believe that **money should be saved,** and spending should be at a minimum while others think they should spend it while they have it since we **can't take money with us** when we die. Often, these conflicts about how financial matters should be handled cause issues within a marriage, especially when bills and debts begin to pile up and it seems as though you have lost control of their money.

Financial secrecy is a big reason a marriage fails. Whoever controls the purse strings controls much of the marriage. If one party feels their spouse is controlling them by money, it's destined to fail. When a couple is considering divorce and finances are their main problem, it is important that they keep in mind the cost of getting divorced. Divorce is not free.

Once all is said and done, both individuals will often feel more in control of their financial life, having the freedom to manage their money the way they see fit. In many cases, how money is handled is a vital aspect of someone's life, so having the ability to spend and save the way they want to is liberating and allows you to feel in control of your future.

Are your dreams on hold? Do you have silent or hidden thoughts and dreams that you can or will not discuss with your spouse for fear of criticism, rejection, abuse or disregard?

Helplessness can result because your **dreams are on hold because your partner doesn't believe in supporting** and nurturing them?

Resentment is painful to endure long term. We all have our aspirations and goals in life, whether it is to have a successful career, write a book, move to a different climate, continue education, travel the world, or settle down and start a family.

Often, when a couple begins to get serious and marry, some of these aspirations end up on the back burner to care for the relationship and the family properly with the hope that in the future those aspirations will once again be attainable.

In some cases, not being able to work toward these goals leads to feelings of resentment between spouses, which can lead to increased unhappiness and arguments. This feeling of being held back will often move one of the spouses to withdraw for a period of time, leave or file for divorce.

When the divorce is complete, that spouse often feels an **incredible amount of freedom and excitement** – without the relationship "holding them back," they are able to get back on track. Pursuing their dreams and achieving their goals, helping them to find a sense of self as well as a sense of fulfillment in their lives. This is also an opportunity for each spouse to find someone else who shares their same aspirations.

Most couples that care deeply about each other are willing to be flexible and consider the needs of their spouse, their children (if there are any) and how vital the desires are to the health and wellbeing of their spouse.
Let's say one spouse is unhappy in a hot, humid climate and wants to live in the cool, dry mountains; or city life is anxiety producing for one spouse and they yearn to live in the country more connected to nature; or one spouse is deeply concerned about finances and wants to be included in all financial decisions and learn more about investing and savings.

Taking the desires of your spouse into consideration and being willing to adapt and adjust is essential to the success of marriage.

This leads us to …once kids come into the picture, there is the added dimension of …

DIFFERENT PARENTING STYLES

Parenting Style Differences: Fun Parent vs Mean Parent.

As any parent will tell you, having children will change the dynamic of a marriage. Adding in the care and support of children can often leave one or both spouses feeling as though they are being neglected. More importantly, some couples have very different ideas of what proper parenting is.

When a couple's parenting styles do not align, it can often cause conflict and resentment between the couple and when it can not be resolved, it often leads to divorce and shared custody of the children. Regardless if parents are married or not, **it is important for the child's well-being that the parents be on the same page when it comes to raising the child.**

While everyone may have different thoughts on what good parenting is, **divorce may be a great opportunity for them to separate their relationship with each other from the way they parent their child.**

Mediation is often an important part of any divorce process and using this time with a professional to work out a custody agreement as well as parenting issues can be of great benefit to both the parents as well as the well-being of the child.

We will dig much deeper into the topic of children and parenting coming up...

And next...

Sexual Incompatibility: Cold as Ice vs Hot to Trot

While this may be an uncomfortable subject to discuss, sexual compatibility is a significant part of any marriage. Humans, by nature, are sexual beings and having a great intimate relationship with your spouse is an integral part of having a healthy, loving marriage. In some cases, the **pressures we feel throughout our lives have a profound effect on our sex lives. Some of these pressures may include:**

1. **Pressure of being married**
2. **Pressure to support spouse/family**
3. **Pressure from a demanding job**
4. **Pressure from health concerns**

The outside factors that cause an individual to feel personal pressure that leads to stress can have a profound effect on how that individual not only feels about themselves but also about their spouse and their relationship in general. In some cases, these **feelings have a direct effect on their sexual performance** with their partner, and when this occurs, it can lead to disappointment and resentment.

When couples divorce for this reason, it is often painful for their egos to endure – one spouse will often feel as though they are not good enough for their former spouse or anyone else. The bright side of getting divorced for this reason is that it allows each spouse to find themselves again and explore what they may or may not want in a partner with whom they will be sexually intimate. Ultimately, it gives them another opportunity to make sure they are fulfilled in all aspects of their relationship not just in the bedroom.

Which can lead to....

Infidelities: OUCH

Infidelity is often a big reason why couples move towards divorce. Any of the reasons we have mentioned, could push a spouse to seek comfort or a relationship outside of their marriage. (This is not a rationalization or proper way to handle it but a fact.) This often leads down a road of pain, disappointment, anger, and resentment for one or both spouses. When infidelity occurs, it is not uncommon for the couple to try and keep their relationship together. Even though the cheating spouse may promise it will never happen again and the cheated-on spouse promises to leave it in the past, the infidelity will in some way, always be present in the relationship.

Divorce due to infidelity is often very liberating for both spouses. The spouse who cheated often feels the freedom to be with whom they wish without feeling any guilt and the cheated-on spouse feels liberated by ending a relationship with someone who did not show them or the marriage the respect they deserved. Both individuals can then seek out new relationships that they find more fulfilling, helping them to avoid the issue of infidelity arising in their lives again. While many people may see these reasons as good reasons to consider divorce, there may also be some areas where you and your spouse can communicate more effectively.

All these issues, when handled in their infancy, are often overcome when couples communicate clearly and respectfully about what they think and how they feel.

In the end, only you can decide whether divorce is right for you. Only you can know what is best for you and your family.

 **I'd like you to consider a few questions to journal on about your thoughts on your discontent.**

1. What are the patterns that keep showing up?
2. What is your gut telling you?
3. Can you see how important this is now?
4. What sounds familiar in your relationship?
5. Are you following someone else's ambiguous advice?
6. Is your gut information solid or in limbo?

Let's now consider… how to share your thought process.

It is never easy to know when to share your internal dialogue.

So, when is the right time to share your feelings?

You will know when the **pain of staying stuck is greater than the fear of change.**

How is this settling in? Are you ready to consider your feelings now that we have worked through your thoughts?

Let's dig a little deeper. Are you ready? I am with you every step of the way towards deeper understanding and greater clarity.

Lesson TWO
Feel Your Feelings

Time to open your journal and consider the following.

How do you let go of the origins of breakup shame and be liberated from toxic feelings of inferiority, humiliation and social embarrassment?

Now it's time to consider …

How to understand why breakups are so hard on the heart, and the critical keys to turning the worst thing that ever happened to you into the absolute best.

 **Learn how to break up better – to leave you and those you love free to move forward with open and fully healed hearts.**

1. How do your feelings affect your life?
2. How do you deal with emotions?
    *   anger?
    *   betrayal?
    *   loss?
    *   shock?
    *   numbness?
    *   control?
    *   confusion?
    *   panic?
3. Are you ignoring your partner? Are they ignoring you?
4. Are you living parallel lives…and for how long?

 Let's get clear on the emotions you are currently feeling. I'll give you a few examples...but don't let my examples be construed as suggestions.

Identify what it is **you** are feeling and name the feelings.

- Feeling disconnect?
- Feeling hostility?
- Feeling avoidance?
- Feeling a lack of intimacy?
- Are you experiencing the silent treatment?

IF you are, how are these experiences making you feel? How are you coping with them?

This may be a good time to pause and sit with those feelings for a bit. This is **not the time to rush** through a thorough understanding and acceptance of your feelings. Physical and emotional feelings are your souls way of getting the attention of your mind to create needed change or recall (memory) experiences that bring you joy.

Now it is time to shift those emotions into the stages of grief, codified by Elizabeth Kubler-Ross in 1969 in her book *On Death and Dying*.

Let's identify the .... Five stages of grief: (This is order isn't linear and it's common to make progress and regress.)

1. **Denial and Isolation**, a sense of LOSS. Common thoughts: This isn't happening. This can't be happening! Life is meaningless. Nothing has value. "I'm fine" is also a common response when people ask how you are.
2. **Anger** sets in ...masking the effects of denial and isolation. Feelings of hatred or repulsion are common. Resentment and blame are common emotions that can lead to feeling guilty for being angry or worse aggressive and violent.

3. **Bargaining/Negotiating**: shifting from a state of hel-plessness and vulnerability is often a need to regain control through a series of "if only" statements: IF only I had tried to be a better spouse. I can do better this time. Just give me one more chance. Guilt also often accompanies bargaining. We start to believe there was something we could have done differently to have helped save our marriage. "What was I thinking?" often runs through the mind.

4. **Depression**: there are typically two types of depression. Sadness and Regret is one. This can last a few days of a month or so, but not longer. The second is a more subtle sense of quiet preparation to separate and say goodbye.

5. **Acceptance**: Not everyone gets to this stage so easily, but it allows us to begin the healing process, see life as valuable and worthwhile again when joy can excitement returns.

Finally, Author David Kessler suggests a sixth stage of grief, *finding meaning in all that has happened.*

It is when we see what we experienced served a purpose. That it taught us a great lesson. That it has brought us a greater sense of meaning and service in your life. It perhaps has shown us how to help others heal, how to see our value and how to find new confidence and truth that was dormant.

There can be a **concern if a stage of grief lasts a long time.**

The difference between normal and elevated stages of grief:

- Elevated means that you move along the stages and take a few steps backwards.
- Elevated means that you move along and stay stuck in one stage for a long time.

We all grieve. It is a natural and healthy process of working through emotional pain. Everyone has different levels of strength, persever-ance and grit to process our emotions. It becomes a challenge when we stay stuck in a stage or skip over a stage …this leads to a danger zone.

You've felt this before…right?

Where are you in the process right now?

If you notice that you are or have been stuck in one stage for an extended period of time, say a month or longer, it is time to seek some counseling or therapy.

Do not go it alone if you cannot move beyond a comfortable amount of time in any stage. It's healthy to know where you are as you move ahead with a better divorce experience.

Do you already have a clearer picture of your marriage?

Let's get clearer on what it is you really want.

Lesson Three
Deciding What You Want

It's time to get clear now on what it is you really want.

No one can do this for you. IF you are the one who wanted the divorce, you may believe you are clear on what it is you really want and need. But do you really know? This is no time to guess.

IF you are the one who was blindsided, you may want to hold on and hope things can get better, or you may want to throw them out of the house and never see them again…but is that realistic?

Maybe it is …maybe it isn't.

What can you live with and what do you need to protect and secure your future?

Here are some things to consider moving forward. Whether we want to see marriage as a legal binding contract and agreement or not…. IT IS!! You were married legally and to end a marriage, it must also be done legally.

1. **Each state has unique divorce laws**. Research them. Read them. Be familiar with them. Get an idea of where you stand with your state's laws.
2. **NOW is the time to know ALL your finances** if you are not aware of them. We will dig deep into this in an upcoming module, but remember your financial health can't be overlooked or taken for granted.

3. **Where you live may change**. Who stays and who goes? Should the martial house be sold? What would an ideal setting be for you and your spouse and if you have **children ...what is in their best interest?**The age of children is a major contribution to this decision.

    - Maintaining routine for children?
    - Are there enough bedrooms?
    - Is there enough space for each member of the family to study, work and rest?
    - How long is the commute from one parent to the other?
    - What is the proximity to the best/most appropriate school to meet the needs of your children in your area?
    - How close are your children's friends if they change neighborhoods or schools?

We will go through a few examples of different models of co-parenting in an upcoming Chapter. But before we do that, **it's time to give some thought to what you believe** *feels* **best**. What do you envision?

 The financial and residential logistics can take some time to work out an ideal and affordable plan...**so it's time to think about what you want.**

1. Is property sold?
2. How is equity divided?
3. Have you tried to FIX communication conflicts?
4. Are you both on board and totally transparent?
5. Are you both financially aware of all your assets and liabilities?
6. Are you on the same page on co-parenting schedules?

This all takes the ability to come to the table in good faith and be willing and able to be open, honest and communicate with respect and consideration for your spouse's needs and feelings as well as what's best for the children.

This I call the "**price of exit**". **We don't all get what we want.**

It sounds beautiful to say…

Know who you are.
Know what you need and want.
Know what you deserve.

But there can be challenges ahead and many things need to be taken into consideration.

It can be a **bit of a gamble and a throw of the dice when we involve lawyers and leave decisions up to a judge to make these life-changing decisions up to them.** There are some critical things to consider before deciding what you want. There are some telltale signs that your relationship, as well as your marriage, are on the fringe.

Making the decision to leave a marriage is scary.

We all fear being alone. We all fear the possibility of not being in a fulfilling relationship. We all fear the possibility of an unknown future. Many people choose to stay together for the children and stick with mediocrity. I settled for a feeling of low-level pain and dissatisfaction instead for many years. I am not the exception.

According to MD Caxton Aderemi Opere research and findings, the medical complications of divorce mimic and replicate the same physical and emotional sensations and feelings in the body. Do not under estimate the effects divorce can have in all areas of our lives. The heart racing, chest tightening, throat closing, headache pounding, muscle weakening sensations in the body are common place for people experiencing the thoughts and procedures before, during and after divorce. This is not to scare you, but to educate you. Have a complete physical and be certain to communicate with you doctor any symptoms you may experience.

Do you believe your mental/emotional/physical health is negatively being effected because of the stress involved in your marriage ? Yet...

Statistics tell us that **85% of people who divorce remarry within five years.**

This proves that most people have the desire to be married.

 **Signs of an unhappy marriage to look for for***

1. You aren't having sex anymore
2. You have little to say to each other
3. You are with each other...but not really with each other
4. You are actively ignoring your gut intuition telling you something is dreadfully wrong
5. You are preoccupied with other peoples' needs and problems
6. The distance between you keeps growing - and you are waiting to get help
7. You fantasize about life without your spouse
8. You've stopped fighting
9. You have one or more relationship destroyers (criticism, defensiveness, contempt, stonewalling)
10. You don't feel heard (and you might not be listening)
11. You are on the verge of having an emotional affair
12. You're going to your friends instead of your partner
13. You don't like spending quality time together...drift away at parties, get home and go to your own corners, you would rather be apart
14. Date nights are a thing of the past
15. You are not each other's priority anymore
16. You're feeling controlled
17. Your partner is unwilling to get help or work on your relationship

* Sourced from Redbook online magazine: 17 Signs You're In an Unhappy — Or Loveless — Marriage - December 2017

 Slow it down. Are any of these behaviors familiar? Now is the time to take out your journal and answer these important questions. Take you time. This is important.

Decide what your non-negotiables are and be creative. **Again... what is your price of exit?**

- What are you willing to let go of?
- What is non-negotiable for you?

You must continue to be **mindful of who you confide in** because friends and family do take sides.

Be **careful and mindful of your demeanor and conversations. Be careful who you trust**.

Taking responsibility for yourself in your emotions, words and actions moving forward is not something to overlook.

Am I right? Can you see how confiding in the wrong person could backfire?
It is always best to keep your emotions in check and your words kind.

It is very common to have a "friend" or family member turn on you. Keep your friends and family in check.

Stay the course and get your journal out to work through what you really want.
Now is the time to do the work.

It's time to get very clear on what you need and what you want NOW.

Get writing!!

NOTES

LESSON FOUR
BEING RESPONSIBLE FOR YOURSELF

Your emotions help dictate your state of mind. Therefore, to keep your state of mind intact, it's necessary to have emotional balance. That way, you can make it through even the most difficult of situations. You can develop emotional well-being, so when difficult times come around, you'll be more prepared to manage them!

These 18 strategies can help you manage your emotions effectively:

1. **Find your support system**. It's easy to experience emotional slumps if you forget that you can experience life with empathy, gratitude and forgiveness. This is especially true when you're making emotionally charged decisions. Always remember that you are totally responsible for perceiving situations in ways that empower you. It's essential to have a few reliable people that can keep you calm, grounded and focused.

2. **Identify friends or family members who can offer objective** input when you find yourself reacting emotionally in a manner that does not serve you. If you do not have objective friends or family get a coach as soon as possible.

3. While your emotions are cross-wired, it helps to have a **wise, non-attached external voice** guiding you towards taking the correct action. Keep in mind, it's best to turn to non-judgmental friends or family who aren't making damaging comments, such as "Why can't you just get over it?" or "Turn the page already."

4. It's healthy to discuss various topics with members of your support system. It helps them see how you think in different situations. **Give your support people the freedom to**

speak honestly and tell you what they see as an impartial observer committed to your happiness.

5. **Face your emotions**. Avoid hiding from undesirable feelings. Facing your emotions is the best way to prevail over them. And the more you practice, the easier it will become to stay calm during emotional situations.

6. If you're brokenhearted, it isn't healthy to pretend otherwise. **Allow the emotional responses to come**. If you feel like crying or screaming, allow yourself to do so. It will help you release negative energy and gain a fuller awareness of your feelings.

7. Once you can vent your emotions, you can then reinterpret your problematic situation in a manner that empowers you. Look for the good in everything and remind yourself that it is ALL good and **every challenge is there for your increased wisdom** and development. What are you learning?

8. **It isn't necessary to over-analyze why you're feeling a certain way**. Identify the source of the emotion and work at processing it instead. Ask yourself, "What do I need to see so this lesson can serve me?" and "Who am I being that is causing this situation to show up around me now? Avoid apologizing for your emotions. Know that your emotions serve as the big red flags telling you that new thinking, actions, or learning are for you.

9. **Celebrate your strengths**. There's no better way to build self-acceptance than by celebrating your strengths. Identify your qualities, talents, and skills that make you feel confident. Remind yourself of how resilient and mighty you are. All too often, we are accustomed to focusing on our flaws – but often overlook our strengths. Acknowledge yourself daily for your courage, commitment, and willingness to take on personal development to be the best you can be.

10. **Your strengths aren't to be brushed aside.** They form your backbone. Create a list of qualities you wish to build upon. Take on the process of consciously developing each one daily. Ask yourself, if I were more (quality), what would I

think, do, or say to demonstrate that quality and project it to the world?

11. **Openly acknowledging your strengths helps you subconsciously believe in yourself.** In turn, you develop a positive emotional state. In your journal, create a list of your current strengths. Acknowledge yourself for each one. Ask yourself, "How can I develop each strength further with a specific course of action?"

12. **Offer emotional support to others.** This helps you work better with your own support team. Assisting others to process their emotions helps you to better process your own. It allows you to be unbiased, fair, and just. As you learn to recognize the ways others fail to perceive life in a way that supports them, you will gain greater insights into how you can do the same in your own life.

13. When you support others, you're required to be straightforward and honest. **Recognizing misperceptions in someone else's emotions can help you recognize the same misperceptions in your own.** We tend to notice the same flaws in others that we see in ourselves. Immerse yourself in personal development, look to champion others to be more confident and your own confidence will increase.

14. **Helping others work through challenges** can help you appreciate their different emotions and, at the same time, build up your own emotional well-being. Support others to separate the facts from the interpretations they made up or bought into that don't support them. As you help others release their negative emotions based on the ways they view situations in self-defeating ways, you will gain greater insight into how to view your own difficult situations from a more empowering perspective.

15. **Surround yourself with positivity.** Maintaining a positive environment is vital to your growth. It helps you focus on positive emotions and enhances the healing process. It's much easier to effectively manage your emotions when you're surrounded by positive energy.

16. **Catch yourself in negative self-talk.** Be willing to release negative thoughts and immediately replace them with empowering, positive thoughts or associations.

17. **Engage in activities you enjoy.** Not to avoid your emotions, but as a tool for developing a positive mindset. As you become more positive, you will develop the tendency to see things in a positive rather than a negative light. Realize that every challenge is there for your personal development, allowing you to grow in self- confidence and emotional resilience.

18. **Your commitment to a positive mindset reinforces your ability to be impartial and fair.** It's easy to be hard on yourself when negative influences surround you. Give up being drawn into other people's stuff. Refuse to take on their negative interpretations. Remember that only you can destroy your self-confidence and only you can restore it. Become a student of personal development and allow every difficult person or problematic situation to become your teacher. Know that each challenge will enable you to grow in wisdom, empathy and self-confidence.

Remember that you have your emotions for a reason!

They help you empathize with others going through similar situations and give you hope.

They also are there to alert you to ways that you are self-sabotaging. To show you opportunities to change your thinking and habits, in ways that offer you greater happiness and an empowered perspective. To help you live in a manner that honors your most important values, in alignment with your vision for your best life.

Use these tips to enhance your emotional well-being. You must remember the big picture.

As important as it is to be responsible for your own emotions, it is also important to NOT take on the emotions of others!!

When we don't take responsibility for our own emotions and we take on the emotions of others, we often use coping mechanisms to mask our inability to handle our emotions or those of others, such as affairs!

There are many kinds of affairs or infidelity.

One that is commonly overlooked is an emotional affair: sharing things with another person that you should reserve for your spouse. IE: you call them instead of your spouse to share good or bad news with FIRST.

You are spending the majority of your time thinking about someone else and they are monopolizing your decisions and intentions, you are keeping financial secrets, perhaps you are buying them gifts and you do not share that with your spouse and

OF COURSE ... flirting, messaging, sharing pictures, cute notes, gifts, poems, songs, memories and mostly all physical touch, including sex. Reaching out to others for gratification and satisfaction will not solve the problems you have at home it will only make them much worse.

Every day you work on developing an empowered attitude will be a day you grow in self-confidence, charisma, and personal power.

There are some deal-breakers!

We are going to jump into those in Lesson Five and they are essential NOT to overlook.

Can you start to see yourself empowering your thoughts and actions now?

Taking responsibility for yourself and your emotions is harder than it sounds. It takes some practice and awareness, but it's worth it!

LESSON FIVE
DEAL BREAKERS

Before we move forward more, it's best to take a few moments to dig deeper into situations in relationships that are of great concern. They are **relationship red flags**: I like to call them deal-breakers. Close your eyes and see if any of these situations are true in your marriage.

1. Reacts to frustration with anger, rage, blame
2. Blames others or circumstances for life situation
3. Tries to control everything, including you
4. Immature, impulsive, and/or irresponsible
5. Emotionally distant or void, aloof
6. Still involved with an ex or says they're "best friends"
7. Wants you to come to their rescue all the time
8. Emotionally unavailable/empty
9. Active addiction, addictive behavior (rationalized as "not a problem")
10. Is pessimistic and negative about things that matter to you
11. Lacks integrity in dealing with people, business, family, money, etc.
12. Judgmental attitude toward themselves & others.
13. Unwilling to self-examine, accept feedback, take responsibility
14. Doesn't keep agreements or appointments
15. What they say about themselves doesn't match reality
16. Emotional roller coaster, recurring or regular emotional drama
17. This isn't what you really want, but you don't want to be alone
18. Changeable, repetitive inconsistent behavior
19. Inability to listen to you or other's opinions
20. You notice yourself trying to change this person to fit what

you want, instead of accepting them for who they are

21. Talks too much (especially about self), monopolizes the conversation
22. Overly quiet, withdrawn. Give you the silent treatment (ghost) if they don't get or hear what they want.
23. Uses other people to communicate to you instead of directly
24. Manipulates the situation to harm you and benefit them
25. Denies your reality. Often says "you're crazy" or "that's not true."
26. Insults you and things you enjoy.
27. Tells you "you'll never change." Makes judgments about your behavior.
28. Flat out lies and/or twists the truth to suit their needs.
29. Creates a smear campaign against you to demean or ruin your reputation.
30. Play the victim. They desire you to feel sorry for them.
31. They refuse/never accept no for an answer.

Now, none of these alone are necessarily a deal-breaker, BUT if you feel a pattern, it's good to notice patterns of behavior. These behaviors break down our self-esteem, our ability to trust yourself and your ability to reason and make decisions.

Now, let's talk a bit about **Narcissistic Abuse Syndrome**. Narcissistic Abuse Syndrome ("NAS") is not a condition that you will find in the DSM. (Diagnostic and Statistical Manual of Mental Disorders) Still, the cluster of symptoms associated with it is now becoming widely recognized by coaches and therapists who are familiar with the traits of Narcissistic Personality Disorder, especially if they are survivors of a toxic relationship.

The symptoms of NAS include the following:

- Feelings of sadness, helplessness, and hopelessness
- Hypervigilance and heightened feelings of fear and anxiety
- Sharp mood swings

- Heightened irritability and proneness to anger
- An overwhelming sense of shame, guilt, and self-blame
- A mindset characterized by shock, disbelief, and denial
- Confusion and difficulty with concentrating or making decisions
- Living in a state of numb acceptance of one's painful circumstances
- Having feelings of being disconnected from the outside world
- Withdrawing from one's family and social circles
- An inability to function - sometimes to the point of losing one's job, home, or children
- Drug, alcohol, food, or shopping addiction
- Not knowing one's purpose in life; daily life seems pointless
- Blocking out parts of one's memories
- Obsessive or ruminating thoughts suicidal thoughts or fantasy and persistent feelings of emptiness
- Feeling unsafe or vulnerable

If you have experienced these feelings, your partner or spouse could likely be a narcissist. I am not a psychiatrist, SO this is **not a diagnosis**, but it is to **open your eyes to these tendencies.**

If this is the case, divorcing such a person will **never be easy.** Learning all you can learn will help you to manage the situation and learn tools to successfully navigate that process much healthier for you and your children.

 **Here are a few Behavioral Patterns to notice:**

- Do you experience Conditional Love: behavior determines love received?
- Silent Treatment: time periods of silence, disregard
- Toxic Shame: feelings of guilt, duty or shame
- Crazy Making: provoking bad feelings through words or actions

- Manipulation: talking others into submission or twisting facts and situations
- Triangulation: using others to communicate through (flying monkeys)
- Minimizing/Demeaning: use of mockery and humiliation
- Gaslighting: Your reality is consistently denied or minimized (what are you talking about?)
- Future Faking: Everything will get better but never does
- Invalidation and criticism: You are not good enough
- Smear campaign: Demean and ruin your reputation
- Play victim: Want others to feel bad for them
- Refusing to take no for an answer
- Ghost you: Disappear for periods of time

There are seven types of abuse:

1. Physical
2. Sexual
3. Financial
4. Emotional
5. Mental
6. Psychological
7. Spiritual

This is a lot of "**tuff stuff**." It's easy to look the other way and want to fix other people, but you can't control others or change them.

1. Get yourself some help
2. Get out if you are in danger
3. There is help
4. Never be afraid to ask for help
5. Call 911, go to a shelter, be safe

The statistics of Domestic violence are NOT good.

Although this online course is **not about domestic abuse**, or abuse in general, if you have experienced any of these deal-breakers, it's crucial that you know you need to be safe, you deserve to be safe, and there is help.

Can you see how important it is to prepare and protect yourself?

Get out your journal and make note of any red flags you are experiencing .

See you in lesson six.

LESSON SIX

HOW TO PREPARE AND PROTECT YOURSELF

Take a look at this list and start to address each suggestion one at a time.

There is no particular order to this list, but it is the best place to begin to prepare for the journey ahead.

How to prepare and protect yourself now.

1. It's essential that you secure your residential property; that includes your computer—security system: "nest" type system. Perhaps you have seen a few brands of very affordable cameras online or in Staples, Office Max type stores? It's not unusual to have mail stolen before, during or even after divorce.
2. Place a camera where your mail is delivered. Consider a PO Box for Legal Documents.
3. Shore up your financial position, so you enter the divorce process prepared.
4. Change ALL login and passwords: email, cell phone, credit cards, bank accounts etc.
5. Open new accounts in your own name.
6. Secure your phone with new passwords or get a new number
7. Establish private communication: NEW email
8. Remain vigilant and aware of subtle nuances.
9. Delete social media (80% of the evidence in divorce comes from social media).
10. Stay OFF social media.
11. Secure all accounts as single/solo account holders.

12. Know exactly where all your valuables are and secure them.
13. Make a list of your valuables.
14. Take pictures of the entire interior and exterior content of your home, paperwork and personal property.
15. Change locks on doors.
16. Do not share keys or codes.
17. Stay calm and quiet. Avoid gossip.
18. Do not change your habits, friends or demeanor

It's not time to be upset or scared…it's time to be smart and safe.

Chapter ONE is done.

How are you feeling? I'd love to know how you are doing.
Know you are not alone.

Time to send me your questions for our online group coaching call OR if you are ready to work with me 1:1…click the link.

REVIEW:
Do Less, Feel More

Let's now review all that we have learned in Chapter ONE.

I know that the six lessons you just learned are loaded with information and emotions to consider. There is a lot to consider.

One more time…there is **no need to rush** this step. It's a good idea to digest all that you have learned and see how it settles. I wish I had. I rushed through this stage and, in some ways ignored it altogether. I knew I was in for a tough road ahead and I just wanted to get over with.

Stage one needs time. Take the time you need to process and prepare.

I cannot impress you enough with the importance of preparation.

If you can save your marriage, you will have a better understanding of the strengths and weaknesses of marriage. You will understand how attitudes and behaviors create discontent and be able to commit to making your marriage stronger and healthier.

BUT if you have stepped a bit closer to knowing or feeling on a deeper level that divorce is your best option…you should feel clearer about your next steps.

Here is what we have accomplished together.

- You should feel clearer about the next steps.
- You should have determined the underlying causes of discontent.
- You should understand the stages of grief and which stage _you're_ in.

- You now know what you want and react better to your partner's wants and desires.
- You should be owning your words and actions and see the benefits of losing a blaming or finger-pointing mentality.
- You should be clear on what is a deal-breaker and know if you have any.
- You should know what to do to keep yourself safe.
- You are clear that social media is not your friend during divorce and commit to taking a much-needed break.
- Regardless if you OR your spouse is the initiator of wanting a divorce, getting clear on the WHY the divorce is up for debate and discussion...there is always a reason you as a couple are in this position. Now is the time to do this work.
- Have you determined your why? Now is your time.

Congratulations! This is tough stuff.

GETTING READY FOR CHAPTER TWO

I want to remind you that you can have a free 45-minute confidential one-on-one discovery call with me to help guide you to where you need to go. Now is the time to book that call with me.

Chapter one isn't easy...so please take some time to congratulate yourself for coming this far. In many ways, the decision to divorce is the hardest. It can sometimes take years to come to this conclusion and it is never one to take lightly.

Statistics show that the average time a person contemplates divorce internally before they dare to communicate it verbally to someone else is TWO YEARS!!

If this is you...you are not alone.

Chapter TWO is where we do a deep dive into figuring out the HOW to divorce.

You simply can't have too much information. I will be asking you to ask yourself a lot of questions. Be sure to have your journal handy. This can be difficult and emotional. I remember being in a state of conflict and not knowing how to feel.

Taking the time to contemplate all that you experience, and feel is not time wasted. You will be glad that you took this time to ask yourself all the important questions to get yourself from the point of panic to composure... or a point of fear to assurance. Having too much information does not exist.

In Chapter TWO, we will walk down the path of figuring out how to divorce.

How much better would that be? Would it increase your chances of success? Let's jump in.

NOTES

2

YOU CAN'T HAVE TOO MUCH INFORMATION

FIGURING THE HERO INSIDE YOU

Getting divorced is a complicated process with many moving parts.

Divorce causes even the most composed individual to experience stress and confusion.

After you've done the preliminary work to determine if divorce is the only option. This we covered in Chapter ONE, and you've nailed down your why, through intention setting and removing judgment. It's time to now explore how you want to proceed and how you want to be able to look back at all this, years from now.

Here are a few facts to consider as we walk down the path together:

1. 1 in 4 divorces are between couples over 50 years old with high assets.
2. The length of your marriage may influence the financial outcome.
3. If you are married just a few years, there is less to consider.
4. If you are married over ten years and have children... then a parenting plan and child support is probably the primary focus.
5. If you have been married over 20 years and have many assets and investments, plus one of the partners has been a stay-at-home parent to raise the children... Alimony is the big consideration. Now that the laws have changed and the payer can't deduct the alimony payment, and the payee doesn't have to pay taxes on it... more payers tend to "settle" without having a tax advantage. (Be sure to consult

with an attorney regarding all alimony laws)

Next, in lesson two, we work through **how to tell the children.**

This is a delicate topic and needs a lot of preparation.

In Lesson Two, we also work through a values exercise that will become the bedrock for your entire divorce.

Creating an affirmation and intention to remind you of the outcome you desire and setting the tone for those times during high stress.

Here are examples of affirmation:

- I believe in, trust and have confidence in myself.
- I learn from my mistakes.
- I never give up.
- I accept what I cannot change.
- I make the best of every situation.

These are the affirmations that got me through my divorce:

- Slow Down…Do Less…Feel More.
- You always get what you settle for.
- I am stronger than I think.
- You can't force a flower to bloom.

I have a dear friend who teaches meditation and recommends keeping affirmations short and simple so you can easily remember them and recite them at the drop of a hat. Here are a few examples:

- I am powerful.
- I release, I let go.
- Everything is perfect and as it should be
- Relax, rest, breathe.

In Lessons Three and Four, we walk down the path of the different methods to divorce and each benefit and disadvantage.

In Lesson Five, we consider all outside factors that could negatively influence your decisions and ultimately the outcome of your divorce.

And finally, in Lesson Six, we walk down an essential step of practicing mindfulness and ways to reduce stress.

This is an essential step towards being prepared and setting a firm foundation for the road ahead. We will practice mindfulness, acceptance and honoring your values.

Can you start to see yourself doing this? How much better would that be? Would it increase your chances of success? I know it will. Take a deep breath and let's dive in together.

NOTES

Lesson One
How to Honor Your Values

This is a deep dive into creating a list of your top values. **"Why is it so important to dissect my values?"**

"I know what I value and what I like." Says most people before they divorce.

You may…but in times of stress and the magnitude of the decisions you will be making as you move forward, it's vital to have them clear and with you always. AND, as you may notice, nothing stands still, and things change. Our values change as we grow and mature into ourselves.

We aren't usually the same people we are when we are 18 or 24 or 30 or 35 …are we? Yes, fundamentally, we are the same.

I suggest here to stop and take the **KOLBE** Index. This will help you learn a bit more about how you act and react to life's situations in both work and relationships. It is a series of 36 questions that will help you understand yourself better and how you deal with stress and decisions making. You can stop the lesson and go take the index now or take it at the end of Lesson One.

The KOLBE index is available from www.kolbe.com and costs $55 (USD) to complete.

Here are Four Colors and a few common traits.

Green= Quick Start (visionary, try new things without hesitation, able to improvise)

Red=Fact Finder (use research in-depth before going somewhere or buying something, ask a lot of questions, need a lot of details before starting a project)

Blue=Implementor (able to read and interpret body language, fixes things instead of calling someone, can build something from scratch)

Yellow=Follow Through (makes a shopping list before going shopping, sometimes referred to as OCD, can organize clothes by color)

You may ask why this is important. It's important because each type will approach divorce differently.

Some will jump in quick. Others will research it, others will try to organize it, others try to fix it.

It's also helpful to know what your spouse is as they will have their way of approaching it.

What are you? What are they? Do they match, or are they oppositional? This insight will help you understand how you approach new tasks and how your spouse approaches new tasks...and this is what divorce is, A NEW TASK.

We will now work on your **core values**. It's important to know that the Kolbe index results are about self-study and self-discovery...not good or bad. You will learn a lot about yourself and your spouse during the entire divorce process. Divorce magnifies the good and the bad in everyone.

It is often said that "criminal law is bad people on their best behavior and family law is good people on their worst behavior".

Our values have a lot to do with our behavior.

 Now, please look through the **List of Values** and complete the following questions.

Take the whole list of "values" and circle the most important 25 to you. What do you value most?
And then once you have them narrowed down...highlight your top 6.

List of Values

Acceptance	Confidence	Excellence
Accomplishment	Connection	Experience
Accountability	Consciousness	Exploration
Accuracy	Consistency	Expressive
Achievement	Contentment	Fairness
Adaptability	Contribution	Family
Alertness	Control	Famous
Altruism	Conviction	Fearless
Ambition	Cooperation	Feelings
Amusement	Courage	Ferocious
Assertiveness	Courtesy	Fidelity
Attentive	Creation	Focus
Awareness	Creativity	Foresight
Balance	Credibility	Fortitude
Beauty	Curiosity	Freedom
Boldness	Decisive	Friendship
Bravery	Decisiveness	Fun
Brilliance	Dedication	Generosity
Calm	Dependability	Genius
Candor	Determination	Giving
Capable	Development	Goodness
Careful	Devotion	Grace
Certainty	Dignity	Gratitude
Challenge	Discipline	Greatness
Charity	Discovery	Growth
Cleanliness	Drive	Happiness
Clear	Effectiveness	Hard work
Clever	Efficiency	Harmony
Comfort	Empathy	Health
Commitment	Empower	Honesty
Common sense	Endurance	Honor
Communication	Energy	Hope
Community	Enjoyment	Humility
Compassion	Enthusiasm	Imagination
Competence	Equality	Improvement
Concentration	Ethical	Independence

Individuality
Innovation
Inquisitive
Insightful
Inspiring
Integrity
Intelligence
Intensity
Intuitive
Irreverent
Joy
Justice
Kindness
Knowledge
Lawful
Leadership
Learning
Liberty
Logic
Love
Loyalty
Mastery
Maturity
Meaning
Moderation
Motivation
Openness
Optimism
Order
Organization
Originality
Passion
Patience
Peace
Performance
Persistence
Playfulness
Poise

Potential
Power
Present
Productivity
Professionalism
Prosperity
Purpose
Quality
Realistic
Reason
Recognition
Recreation
Reflective
Respect
Responsibility
Restraint
Results-oriented
Reverence
Rigor
Risk
Satisfaction
Security
Self-reliance
Seless
Sensitivity
Serenity
Service
Sharing
Significance
Silence
Simplicity
Sincerity
Skill
Skillfulness
Smart
Solitude
Spirit
Spirituality

Spontaneous
Stability
Status
Stewardship
Strength
Structure
Success
Support
Surprise
Sustainability
Talent
Teamwork
Temperance
Thankful
Thorough
Thoughtful
Timeliness
Tolerance
Toughness
Traditional
Tranquility
Transparency
Trust
Trustworthy
Truth
Understanding
Uniqueness
Unity
Valor
Victory
Vigor
Vision
Vitality
Wealth
Welcoming
Winning
Wisdom
Wonder

Define the top values you want to honor. Now that you have your top six values, I recommend you write these six words on an index card and keep it with you anytime you are experiencing stress and getting wrapped up in confusion and other people's drama.

You will find this very useful to keep these close to you when you get wrapped up in the drama and confusion ahead.

For example: Let's say one of your top 6 values is authenticity… and you are in a situation where you are bending the truth or trying very hard to be as others want you to be and not really "being you". You will suffer in the long run if you are not honoring your values.

How does it feel to clearly know your top values?

Can you see how knowing these and having them clearly in your sight will assist you along the way in making better decisions? And to get you through times of turmoil and confusion?

There will be times when you need to know what is of importance and value to you.

Now it's time for some reality testing. **What is reality testing you ask?**
It's another way of checking in with yourself to see how your decisions are possible or not possible by testing whether what is important to you can be tested and proven to become a reality.

You will need your journal.

 *Reality Test Questions:*

- What is happening now that tells you this is important to you?
- What are you tolerating by not moving on this issue?
- What have you attempted to resolve this?

- What feedback are you getting from your environment, health, friends, family, etc.?
- Who on your team can help?
- What obstacles are in your way?
- What are your beliefs about achieving this outcome?
- What can you learn from someone who has already achieved this?

What are your options?
- What options are available to you?
- What could you do if you were without fear?
- What could you do if you were not answerable to anyone?
- What could you do if time or money was not a constraint?
- What could you do if the most important outcome was to learn more about yourself?
- What do you need to believe to open your options even more?
- How are your values being expressed or not being expressed by your actions, thoughts and feelings?

Now that you are more familiar with your values and what is important to you and how you see the world...

Can you see how this will be an invaluable tool to help you stay calm, focused and determined to honor your values? No matter what lies ahead in the future we always have options. At times the only option we can control is our reaction to the situation...but nonetheless that is still an option.

It's now time to think about how to tell your children and when to tell them.

This was one of the hardest days of my life...I'm here for you. I understand how difficult this is.

Lesson Two
How to Tell the Children

This is a sensitive and very important topic. Why?

Because children are in our care. They are our responsibility. They are innocent. They are not to blame. They are vulnerable. They are growing and we are their examples.

Parents are never perfect. Parents are human too, but it is essential that we consider them in all of our choices.

There is no greater message to begin your divorce with, than to be sure the kids know the following.

Parents who stray from this message, can forget the impact and get lost in the process of confusion and drama. If you find yourself doing that ...remember **you can get back on track**. The messaged wording is unique to all situations and families, but here is the message they need to understand and hear...repeatedly.

1. You are, and always will be, loved by Mom and Dad.
2. You are, and will continue to be, safe.
3. You are not to blame for any of this.
4. Mom and Dad will always be your Mom and Dad.
5. This is about change, not about blame.
6. Everything is going to be okay.

There is no reason to give them any more than this. Just keep on message and on task and reassure them every chance you get. And every time they appear to be sad or need reassurance. Just restate these facts in any way and every way you find appropriate given the situations and questions.

When is the **right time** to tell the children?

This is a hot topic that many parents disagree on. There are a few things to consider…

- Age of the children?
- The personality of each child?
- Will the children be moving?
- Are they aware of conflict?
- Is there abuse?
- Are they attached to one parent more than the other?
- Is there hostility between the children and one parent?

I refer to my **Parenting Expert Rosalind Sedacca**. She is the founder of the **Child-Centered Divorce Network**. Her expertise and mission are to enlighten parents, educators and society about the emotional and psychological effects of divorce on children.

Rosalind writes…

"It is not divorce itself that negatively affects our children. It is the parent's approach to divorce that determines whether their children will be angry, insecure, frightened or in other ways emotionally scarred from the divorce experience."

Rosalind continues…

"We encourage all divorcing parents to remember their roles and responsibilities towards their children. In that way, we can prevent unnecessary pain, suffering, confusion, guilt or shame for them at this difficult time in their lives. We are passionate about enlisting the legal, therapeutic and educational communities around the world to bring a heightened awareness about ways to create the most positive and harmonious outcomes for families transitioning through divorce."

"Our goal is to spread the word that when parents' divorce, their children need them more than ever. I want to help you avoid the mistakes that create emotional pain for your children. We are here to help you stay out of the courts whenever possible. I encourage you to be a compassionate, loving parent who understands your children's need for both their parents in their lives."

Refer to her website for information and tools to help you create a child-centered divorce.

For more information on working with Rosalind, you can find her at www.childcentereddivorce.com

Ask yourself: Do you love your children more than you hate your spouse? How much is TMI?
Details. Criticism. Money. Past. It's all a NO...NO...NO...NO.

You can enroll in a parenting class in MOST states. They are not always the best parenting classes...but do partake, learn what you can and at the very least, you may meet some other fabulous people who are also struggling through the journey of divorce and co-parenting.

Call your children's school and make an appointment with their teachers, coaches and guidance counselors. If your spouse agrees to go with you great...if not go alone. Tell them you are concerned about your child's education and wellbeing if you do decide to divorce or you are divorcing and let them know how to communicate with you about anything they find and see anything unusual.

If you find your children giving you the cold shoulder, talking back, disrespecting you, lying to you, keeping secrets, whispering to their siblings (don't tell mom/dad), or other telltale signs ...you may be experiencing **alienation**. (If so, it's time to get help with professionals and document everything.)

You may need proof that your spouse is attempting to poison the children against you so they do not have to pay child support, alimony, share parenting time etc. Or express any other feeling of anger, control, resentment or hatred they are feeling for you, using the children to get back at you. This is NO joke. Stay calm. Be kind. Get help from professionals. Lashing out is the worst thing you can do. They will gaslight you (deny your reality) and try to make you feel crazy and selfish.

Parenting plans are not easy to create BUT there are wonderful templates that are available to you to allow you to see different options for school, holiday, vacations, special events and summer vacation. I have several on my website that Divorceify created. They will allow you to **visualize joint physical custody** as well as primary custody.

It is usually best for parents to share 50/50 time with the children, but that is not always possible.
Much will also depend on the age of the children. Typically when children are 14 they have a say in where they reside in the eyes of the laws in most states.

Parents who have jobs that require travel may have very different needs. Parents who work from home may have different needs. The ages of the children will also dictate the needs of the children. Every family is unique and so is their parenting time plan. Templates save time and frustration and allow both parents to see many options to consider that are possible and better for the children.

 Things to consider

1. Distance between homes
2. Nesting: kids stay in same house and parents shift
3. Ability of parents to be civil and respectful to each other
4. Ability of parents to communicate effectively
5. Support system in place of both parents
6. Financial means
7. Use of **Parenting APPS** such as OurFamilyWizard, AppClose, WeParent, TalkingParents, coParenter, Truece and Fayr

Raising children while contemplating, surviving and recovering from divorce requires organization, planning, commitment and a calm unconditional demeanor.

This is the time to call in the experts if you have children and create a plan.

One that is in the best interest of the children and is one that both parents can live with.

Now that we worked on what is best for the children, it's time to determine what is right for you.

Nod your head if you think this would be beneficial for you and your family.

LESSON THREE
How to Decide What is Right for You

At all costs, **consider** creating a team that keeps you out of lawyers' offices and court proceedings.

Lawyers are best when they are the last ones to enter the conversation. That is if there are NO deal breakers!!

Before you walk down the path straight into an attorney's office, be sure you **understand ALL your options**.

IT DOES TAKE BOTH partners to be willing, and able, to disclose all financial information and avoid all attacking and blaming tactics for a couple to divorce respectfully and successfully. This is possible. BUT if for some reason this is not the case, do not give up hope. I am proud to be a vetted professional, board and chair member of Amicable Divorce Network. The next lesson explains the six different approaches to the divorce process. These include DIY, mediation, collaboration, arbitration, litigation and the ideal, amicable.

Do still consider mediation. If you go into mediation with an open mind and are willing to make some concessions and negotiations, you are always ahead of depending on a lawyer and locking up litigation. BUT if you come to an impasse for whatever reason, do not see yourself as a failure. There is a reason we have a judicial system and there are times when you do not have any other choice.

This situation is rare. If you are here, your spouse may well fall into the category of a person with narcissistic traits or a high conflict personality. Some traits you may see include a lack of empathy, feeling entitled to a fight, hiding finances, thinking only of themselves and want to "win" at all costs.

They are typically angry that you are no longer cooperating with "their rules," and you are "bucking their system" (it's their system and not one of reality) and asking for relief of actual fair justice.

They are usually angry that you are not serving their needs anymore. You once served their needs and they are sad, angry, resentful and truly ANGRY you have learned to stand up for yourself and demand fair, honest, open treatment, particularly when it comes to finances.

They believe you have no right to want or need anything and they have every right to demand you go away and get nothing. They usually hire lawyers that like to push papers, file motions, complaints and appeals. It is a long, expensive and exhausting process.

What is right and what is necessary is not always the same thing. Getting legal advice and knowing the law is much different than hiring a "bulldog" who will drag this out beyond all reasonable measure just for billable hours (or worse minutes) and end up tearing you and your family apart.

Each method of divorce has an energy attached to it!!

It's essential to connect the dots between your values and the type of divorce method you choose. In lesson four, we will dig much deeper into the different methods. This is important before you jump into one of them without knowing the pros and cons of each.

Lesson Four
How to End a Marriage

Generally, the moment you get an attorney involved in the day to day process, it will cost a lot of money and create an adversarial situation. An attorney is educated and trained to seek the benefit of ONE party only. They are trained to win at all costs and serve ONE party. The language is more adversarial and accusatory. It never sets up a kind and respectful atmosphere and energy where both parties' needs are considered.

With that said, attorneys are necessary to educate you about the laws in your state, file paperwork with the courts and check over agreements to be sure all the paperwork is filled out and filed correctly.

There are **six methods to consider** when deciding to end your marriage in divorce.

1. DIY (self-directed)
2. Mediation
3. Collaboration
4. Arbitration
5. Litigation
6. Amicable

As a rule, do not consider DIY, amicable, mediation or collaborative methods if

1. You suspect your spouse is hiding assets/income
2. Your spouse is domineering, and you are afraid to speak up or question facts or figures
3. There is abuse of any kind
4. There is addiction involved

The day you file for divorce is usually your Date of Separation (DOS). This date will dictate how funds are used. Changing any financial documents and or funds is not permitted by law after this date.

I will take you through an explanation of methods one by one and explain:

1. Time frame
2. Cost
3. Emotional stress
4. Trauma on family and children

METHOD 1: DIY

DIY can be as short as a month if all the financial preparation is complete. Plus both parties have equal and full access to documents and both parties are transparent and come in good faith.

- Filing online is inexpensive and fast
- It is possible to file yourself at the courthouse in your city or town with no attorney
- It usually is a good idea to have an attorney look over your financial statements and agreement to be certain everything is filled out properly.

New lawyers who recently passed the bar exam are hungry and will usually consider pro-bono (free) work.

Most attorneys also consider some pro-bono work. You can also go online and research free legal counsel in your area. Many groups, unions, and some businesses have attorneys who work for them and may even consider pro bono work. This is the least stressful IF all goes well. But if something is overlooked, or one of the spouses is hiding facts, this could be a problem down the line especially, if the information is discovered after the fact.

You could end up in court, after all. It could be messier and more expensive than if you went to court in the first place. DIY has less conflict, less drama and less trauma.... again, that is if all goes well and BOTH parties are entirely transparent. This is tricky. Because one of the most common reasons couples divorce is because of money conflicts. It's challenging to trust someone during the divorce if you feel or know they are keeping financial secrets.

If you have been married a short period of time, (under five years) have few assets, both independently employed, no children, little debt and both want to end the marriage DIY is a good way to go.

METHOD 2: MEDIATION

Mediation is a neutral process where both parties are in control of the outcome and they get to steer the boat. A mediator is a facilitator of the process that allows each party to express their needs and desires. Both parties need good-faith negotiation, and an impasse could result. If that is the case, the parties reserve the right to continue later or begin to litigate, although 70% of cases do come to an agreement.

Mediation is a private, confidential process that is controlled by the parties and not the lawyers or courts. All parties are bound to confidentiality and must sign a confidentiality agreement. All mediators have their own style and demeanor, but follow a strict code of ethics and requirements. Impartiality and confidentiality are essential. Both parties are usually represented by counsel ...but it's not necessary. OR they both agree to have the agreement created during mediation looked over by counsel, after the mediation process to check for clarity, compliance and fairness.

Attorneys here keep their client's best interest at heart but could start to create some tension or conflict if one side or both do not feel like they are being respected or heard. It takes a lot of effort to see the outcome and its long-term benefits, instead of demanding what you want. Mediation is usually the best situation for the children as you and your spouse are in control of making decisions that will affect all your lives forever.

Mediation itself typically takes one or two eight-hour sessions. This can be a shorter time IF only areas of conflict need to be worked on, for example, parenting plan, child support, household items, etc.

After an agreement is created, the mediator or the attorney/s write up the agreement that both parties must sign.

This agreement is given to a lawyer to write up the legal document, that is presented to the judge in court. The judge will hear and ask both parties if they created the agreement of their own free will, that they read it, understand it, that they have no questions, that they had the advice of counsel. They know it will be a legal binding contract and the dissolution of their marriage.

Mediators typically charge an hourly rate. The average rate is $150-$350 an hour. Some mediators may offer a mediation package price for both parties to share.

More and more networks and organizations are working together (Divorceify, Fairway Divorce Solutions, Amicable Divorce Network, National Association of Divorce Professionals, DivorceTown USA, Divorce Force, Vesta etc) to offer a team approach to making divorce more affordable, less adversarial and more efficient.

We will dive deep into who these other professionals may be in Chapter Five. You many need none of them or all of them.

If the mediator is associated with a firm, they may also charge for office space, office support, separate caucus space, lunch, coffee etc.

METHOD 3: COLLABORATION

Collaborative Practice of Law. VS a Collaborative Team Approach

In **Collaborative Law**, both parties are represented by counsel. Both parties and their attorneys MUST agree to stay out of court. It is the good faith intention to stay out of court. Both parties agree that their attorneys will come together with them present to discuss and go over the terms of the proposed agreement. This can take some time, perhaps weeks or months based on the financial transparency and conflict. Lawyers charge hourly. The average costs are $350-550 an hour. It can be costly but less than litigation.

IF ONE or BOTH parties want to pull out of the process, the negative aspect is… BOTH parties must use NEW attorneys and all the evidence and agreements are not permissible. You must start again from day one. This can be shorter, less traumatic on the children, but still adversarial and costly.

You can also each have an attorney to negotiate out of court. It doesn't always have to rise to the level of collaborative divorce.

In a Collaborative "Team" Approach, professionals and experts from every aspect of divorce work together as a team, in one location or separately but close. An attorney who works for the team is available for legal advice but is not controlling the process. The client is in control of the process with the financial, mediation, taxation, residential, parenting, mental health team member support, guidance, coaching and results. A flat rate is usually charged at the beginning of the process upon intake. The average is $5000-8000 USD.

This allows the parties to meet with each of the team members to create a satisfactory and less adversarial plan. If more time is needed for mediation, financial planning, real estate, CPA, insurance, parenting plans, child support, emotional support, eldercare, career transition coaching, etc. expert professional services are there to collectively create a divorce agreement that is unique and custom to fit their needs and goals. The team is well versed in each other team member's expertise and works for the benefit of the client's needs.

METHOD 4: ARBITRATION

In cases of arbitration, BOTH parties are represented by counsel And ONE Arbitrator resides over a final decision in the case. The decision is final, and the decision cannot be appealed. Very rarely does divorce end in Arbitration, but it is essential to know all the methods. If it goes "your" way, you may be happy. If it doesn't go "your" way, you may be angry. But I'll tell you this…both of you will be miserable and co-parenting will be hell and your kids will be traumatized. It's less expensive and shorter than litigation but just as stressful.

METHOD 5: LITIGATION

And finally, Litigation. You are at the mercy of a complicated legal system, long court proceedings, clogged court calendars, attorney and judge conflicts, stressful "discovery" (collection of the facts), expensive billing, and your children caught in the middle.

But there are times when it's your **ONLY choice**. IF your spouse is hiding financial information, keeping secrets, acting abusive and controlling and refuses to be transparent, respectful and cooperative, you have no other choice.

The courts exist for a reason: to protect the rights of people. To give you a secure place to be heard. To force compliance and accountability and it all has a price. The judge, or in some states a jury, makes the decision. And unlike Arbitration, the decision can go to the Appeals Court, which takes more time, more money and more drama. I have seen appeals take up to five years and cost upwards of another 100K. The cost can be immense in money, time, relationships and heartache.

METHOD 6: AMICABLE

This process is centered around the attitude of the parties and their desire to resolve their family law matter efficiently and with low conflict. The parties must both agree to utilize the Amicable Divorce process and professionals in the Amicable Divorce Network who are vetted and trained. The parties may or may not have their issues worked out at the outset of the case, but if there are disagreements, they agree to use alternative dispute resolution means (such as mediation) to resolve differences instead of the court system. Parties exchange necessary information and documents. There is a streamlined process to reduce conflict and cost.

You must decide which method is best for you and your family based on the amount of disclosure, communication and conflict.

I call it the "**Price of Exit**". Court and litigation may be your price of exit as it was for me. It's long, draining, expensive, confrontational and emotional, to say the very least. And as an ending caveat … IT IS TIME TO START PUTTING SOME MONEY ASIDE TO BE ABLE TO AFFORD A DIVORCE. If you believe that a divorce is in the cards and you think that it is not going to be cooperative and respectful…plan now.

Hope for the best but plan for the worst!! If things work out, you will have an excellent vacation account or an IRA. Remember, knowledge is power. When you know better, you do better. You want a better divorce. You can have a better divorce but only if you plan and learn your best options.

In Lesson Five, we will uncover mitigation outside influence.

NOTES

LESSON FIVE
HOW TO MITIGATE OUTSIDE INFLUENCES

Let's now consider how your personal story and experience can play a role in your divorce. It's never easy to separate our history from our marriage. Be sure to use your online journal now or grab your pen and paper journal.

 **Questions to answer:**

1. Did you come from a divorced family? What was its impact on you?
2. Did you have friends who were from divorced families? How did that affect you?
3. Did you grow up with messages about what divorce meant? What were those messages?
4. Did you discuss divorce with your spouse when you were dating?
5. Is your spouse from a divorced family?
6. What messages did their experience bring into your marriage?
7. What role, if any, did religion play?
8. What role did TV/Movies play in your ideals about divorce?
9. What emotions and fears do you have about what others will think about you and your children?
10. Are you afraid of "what the neighbors will think?"
11. Are you afraid of "what your family will think?" Or your spouse's family?
12. Are you able to let go of other's opinions and judgments?

Continue to contemplate and journal your experiences and your spouse's experiences with divorce and how they have affected you and your marriage.

The answers to these questions will help you understand how the **opinions of others keep us stuck,** make our decisions for us or guilt and shame us into wanting something other than what we believe we need and want.

How do you let go of the origins of breakup shame and be liberated from toxic feelings of inferiority, humiliation and social embarrassment?

How do you step into your power and know what it is you need and want and not that of others?

If the answers to these questions, feel difficult and unimaginable, take time to sit with the feeling and visualize your life with compassion and empathy...as if it were a dear friend's life and not your own. We tend to have more compassion for others than we do for ourselves.

If you have never done this before, this will be very challenging.
Take a deep breath to accept how your marriage truly is and how it will be when you're on the other side.

It's now time to introduce you to a brilliant writer that helped me see how I was making my decisions.
Not only my divorce decisions but all of the choices I made in my life.

Bronnie Ware: The Top Five Regrets of the Dying is a book worth reading at any time, but particularly before divorce.

The number ONE regret of the dying.

1. **I wish I'd had the courage to live a life true to myself, not the life others expected of me.**

2. **I wish I hadn't worked so hard**

3. **I wish I'd had the courage to express my feelings.**

4. **I wish I had stayed in touch with my friends.**

5. **I wish that I had let myself be happier.**

Regret is a terrible thing, particularly when it comes to divorce and the work we choose to do.

Living your life on OTHER'S TERMS ... OTHER'S CHOOSING!!

This is never a good way to live our life.

Universal emotions associated with regret are: Feeling Used. Resentful. Sad. Unfulfilled. Angry. Bitter.

I believe that cancer and other illnesses (autoimmune: IE your body is fighting you) set in when you are living in a state of long term stress and living a life just to please others and make them proud of you by their definition of expectations. **You can never make others happy being something other than who you are.**

May years ago, I read a quote that made me cry when I read it because I was living the opposite of it.

It is better to be hated for what you are than loved for what you are not.

I was loved for what I was not because I smiled and pretended I was happy and content. To make others like me and love me and accept me and adore me and want me and anything else I felt I was lacking. I wanted to do what they liked or needed from me so they would approve of me and accept me.

How sad.

Living like that makes you miserable and if you live like that over some time, it makes you sick...emotionally ill and physically ill.

Please consider this when you are making your decisions. You won't be sorry you did the work now.

In Lesson Six, I'm going to teach you: MINDFULNESS.

It's a game-changer.

LESSON SIX
HOW TO PRACTICE MINDFULNESS.

What is mindfulness? Is it the state of our mind being full? I like to call it "awarefulness" (I know …it's not a real word.) In other words, Mindfulness is the … awareness and expertise in and understanding that we were in control of our emotions vs. our emotions control us.

Let's experiment and give mindfulness or awareness a try!!

1.   Settle into a comfortable seat
2.   Close your eyes
3.   Relax your eyes in their sockets
4.   Create more space between eyebrows and eyelashes
5.   Soften your face, your jaw
6.   Allow your tongue to hover and float freely in your mouth

Connect to the five qualities of breath

1.   Deep: Is your breath deep down into the lowest part of your belly and filling your diaphragm?
2.   Smooth: Is your breath smooth like silk with no jagged edges?
3.   Even: Is your inhalation and exhalation the same length? Count to 5 for inhale and 5 for exhale.
4.   Circular: Visualize a circle in your mind and allow the breath to have no ending and no beginning.
5.   Silent: You shouldn't hear your breath. For this practice, it is best to have your breath silent.

Optimal Breath Cycle: will lower your heart rate, slow your pulse and soothe your sympathetic nervous system.

1. 60-second breath cycle is the minimum amount of time you should practice four times a day. (IWatch has the Breath feature on it)
2. Inhale for 5 seconds
3. Exhale for 5 seconds
4. Repeat 6 times for a full 60 seconds.

Notice your pulse/heart-rate slowing down.
Notice your mind focusing on your breath and nothing else.
Notice the calming effect this practice has on your neurological system.
Your muscles relax. Your mind and your breath become one.

Do this anytime you feel stressed, attacked, frustrated or angry.

While I was in the courtroom, I would practice this while I was waiting to hear from the judge.
When I was on the phone with someone who was attacking me.
When I was about to see someone who was mean, critical, controlling or narcissistic.
Anytime I needed to unplug from my mind and connect to my inner voice of compassion and strength.

 Next, **visualize and contemplate on an issue you've struggled with for a long time and include HOW LONG you have been struggling with it.**

1. What emotions are you experiencing and name them?
2. What are some common thoughts that show up when you think about this situation?
3. What emotions do you experience when you think these thoughts?

It may be one thought or several thoughts (i.e., I can't handle/stand this. Why is this happening to me? I'm a failure. Nothing goes right for me. What if I don't get past this? What if I lose everything?)

Let's now explore how your mind works.

All humans have four parts of our mind. The first three usually do not serve us in times of stress and decision making.

1. Our five senses and our response to them
2. Our attachment to our identity (ego) Our "I AM"ness.
3. Our memory, impressions, patterns and habits
4. Our discriminating intellect or our ability to discern and reflect (sometimes called intuition or instinct)

Only the fourth part of our mind can connect to the voice of our self, our soul or our spirit. This is the part of us that already knows what we desire.
Our breath is the conduit to access this part of our self. Practice it and you will have easier access to it.

Continue to breathe smoothly and deeply and visualize the situation and the emotions attached to it. Continue to visualize as I ask you about some contemplative thoughts.

1. **What strategies do you use to try to control/get rid of/ fix the distress (aka difficult emotions and thoughts) that you experience as a result of this situation?** I.e. some people drink or take drugs to make themselves feel better, some people avoid doing something or procrastinate. Others try to reduce their interpersonal distress by avoiding people... even a loved one.
2. When you take a close look, you may notice that some of the things you do to try to get rid of distress don't work at all. The strategy does not work.
3. The strategy that works in the short term.

4. The strategy that works in the long term.
5. The strategy that can be harmful to yourself and/or others?
6. The strategy that cost you something. It has proven to move you further away from what you value.

Now slowly return to your breath and be mindful and aware of what you are feeling. Slowly open your eyes and return to the space around you and become aware of the space around you.

Do you see things differently? This can take time and practice. Be patient and compassionate with yourself.

 **Grab your journal** and write for a few minutes about that experience and any takeaway you have.

Course students can also use the downloadable PDF worksheet to help you journal and identify the strategies that take you away from what you value most.

Six Options:

1. What options are available to you?
2. What could you do if you were without fear?
3. What could you do if you were not answerable to anyone?
4. What could you do if time or money was not a constraint?
5. What could you do if the most important outcome was to learn more about yourself?
6. What do you need to believe to open up your options even more?

Now let's consider stepping into the future a bit...

Ten forward-thinking questions

1. Which one of your options will bring you one step closer to your desired outcome?

2. What actions do you need to take?
3. Is there anything you need to do before taking these actions?
4. How do you know that you are committed?
5. By what date will you have completed the action(s)?
6. What resources will you need to do this?
7. Do you need to tell anyone about your commitment?
8. What are your obstacles? How will you address them and when is your deadline?
9. On a scale of 1-10 (1=poor, 10=excellent) How do you rate yourself on each of the following? Commitment to action, Enthusiasm, Excitement, Certainty
10. What do you need to change to answer all the above with a 10?

Let's now take a look at

Negative and Positive Labels: we internalize and send to ourselves.

- Negative …I am the worst at….
- Positive …I am the best at…
- We label ourselves continuously.
- We think of ourselves in positive ways (honest, strong, good parent)
- Or we think of ourselves in negative ways (untrustworthy, lazy, temperamental)

 **It's time to think of the labels you often apply to yourself and write them down in our journal.**

At my worst, I am…. Top 8.
At my best, I am… Top 8.

Why is it important to do this?

There will be times when you get down on yourself when things are not going well, when there is conflict or when you simply feel sad. It's essential to always stay on the best side and not the worst side. Let your imperfections go and allow yourself to focus on the things that you do well and are best at.

Now let's step into how our thinking shapes our outcome.

 **Five Growth Questions:**

1. Describe the current situation.
2. How is this challenging you now?
3. How would you like the situation to be?
4. How is this important to you, your purpose and your values?
5. What is the specific outcome you are looking for once this is resolved?

Be sure to do all four parts of practicing mindfulness

1. Options
2. Forward Thinking
3. Negative and Positive Labels
4. Growth

As we wrap up Chapter Two, take a moment to think of how far you have come. How much you have learned and how much more aware you are of who you are and what you desire?

Phew…who knew practicing mindfulness would be so much work but so rewarding?

REVIEW
TAKE CONTROL

1. The impact on the children is based on what they see and what they hear.
2. How you react and process is key to how children will heal and recover from divorce.
3. Your values play a pivotal role in how you proceed... and succeed.
4. Take the time you need to decide what is BEST for you and the outcome you desire and deserve.
5. A lawyer and a courthouse are not the only way to proceed when you are ready to end your marriage.
6. How can you best find your way around outside influences?
7. Always be aware of your options.
8. Do you acknowledge and accept your emotions as they come to the surface?

One step at a time... this chapter has you taking control. In Chapter Three, we address all the steps we need to take before filing for divorce. Coming up next!

There is something to be said about trust. Trust the process. But what process is it? The law? Marital honor? Family Obligation? Knowledge is power and the more you know, the better!

You can never be too prepared. It's also essential to secure your financial and personal papers NOW.

NOTES

3

IT'S OK TO LET YOUR OCD KICK IN: YOU CAN NEVER BE TOO PREPARED

WHAT TO DO BEFORE FILING

You Can Never Be Too Prepared

Now is our time to dig deep and know what to do BEFORE you file for divorce. The issue that is embedded in the law-even in no-fault states or in uncontested divorce… is that ONE of the parties must be the plaintiff and one is named the defendant. Isn't it CRAZY?? I mean really. Who committed the crime? Who is to blame? NO ONE. This isn't criminal law…it's family law. Well, it is what it is… so let's deal with reality. Ignorance is not bliss. There is no excuse not to know the law.

- YOU can do your research.
- YOU can be prepared.
- YOU can be organized.
- YOU can gather your facts.
- YOU can have a copy of every document.

It all starts with a complete financial disclosure document.

BOTH parties are required IN ALL 50 states to provide a fully transparent financial statement. EACH state's form is slightly diffe-rent. You can get these forms at a courthouse or online. Know your budget details and complete the form thoroughly. I know it's a pain to recall monthly dry-cleaning bills or to figure out what you spend on "entertainment," but you must take the time to do it!!

Speaking with lawyers and reading legal documents can be scary and intimidating. Do all the research you can do. You can never have too much information. Gather your evidence: Paystubs, tax returns, insurance policies, etc. Schedules, photos, cards, gifts, etc. When in doubt, keep it!!

You must have a budget. We will walk down the financial road more and establish the importance of having a budget. Get familiar with "**Lawyer Speak**," even though the language feels foreign. Google common lawyer lingo and study it. You don't need to memorize them all but be familiar.

Here are a few common ones:

> Assumptions
> Implications
> Leading statements

For example, think about Bill Clinton and Monica Lewinsky, "I did not have sex...." What the definition of sex?

If you are not sure of what something means, **refrain from replying.**

ADVOCACY IS IMPORTANT

Begin a list of who you believe understands your position and case IF you need someone to back you up with facts and evidence. IE. The best interest of children, work-related issues, parenting etc.

NOW is the time to make sure you have a Planner or Calendar and start using a Journal!!!

One of the reasons I require you to have an online or paper journal is to teach you how to have and use a journal.

Assuming you already keep appointments and contacts in your phone, it's important to document your emotions, goals and dreams in a planner or journal. Just a reminder IF You still have not created an account in Penzu ...DO IT!

Paper is great too! Whatever works for you. **Never assume you will remember anything. You won't!**

 Here are a few **categories to create in your planner** that you will want to make a note of that are not direct communication with professionals, but having them all in one spot will be very helpful.

1. Financial payments that are late, ie, child support, or spousal support. Keep track of the date you were supposed to receive it, the date you actually received it and if you NEVER received it.

2. Expenses that your soon to be ex (STBX) is supposed to reimburse you for. (medical costs, utilities, maintenance, real estate taxes...etc.)

3. All spending you incur to prove your budget (along with bank statements and credit card statements)e

4. Unusual or concerning activity, behavior and communication. (where, who, when and if anyone else witnessed it too)

5. Parenting time changes or alterations. Keep note of all dates and deviations.

6. All verbal attacks, criticisms and passive aggressive communication. Make note if the children were present, within earshot, if others were present of if you were alone.

7. Any parenting irregularities and failures: IE late or early exchanges, no shows, interference, complaining. And if the other parent also participated in or attended school conferences, sporting events, plays, doctor appointments...etc.

8. What your children say, repeating what the other parent said or told them.

9. If you are still living together: it's helpful to LOG the details of parenting functions: bathing, hygiene, meal preparation, drove to school, help with homework, signed teacher and doctor notifications, filled out camp and medical records.

10. If one parent is often missing, late, not home...make note of what time they left and when they returned home.

11. **Make a note of** ANYTHING else that feels noteworthy or important. Trust me...you will forget. You may never

need it or look at it again…but it could be important and will save you so much stress trying to recall when your mind is overwhelmed and in a state of fight or flight.

Your mind is full of information, emotions and thoughts. To keep it straight, it's best to have ONE place to keep it all straight.

Lesson ONE
Ignorance is NOT Bliss

There is no bliss in ignorance, and it will cost you a lot to pretend you are "all set," or you can do it all by yourself. It's time to dig into the details!! What are the most important key pieces of information that you need to know?

Do you know your credit score? If so, check again. Most people who are going through divorce experience a significant drop in their credit score. Some of the reasons your credit rating may go down 1) Change address. 2) Close accounts 3) Request new credit cards 4) Cancel credit cards 5) loss of insurance

Request and/order a copy of Experian, Equifax and TransUnion credit report. Scan through it and see if you see any discrepancies. Call them to dispute. Document your conversations. Be diligent with your payments and spending habits.

Now that you have a system to collect and record your appointments, contacts, goals and emotions, it's time to create a system to store your paperwork, receipts and communications

- Collect
- Gather
- Take Pictures of EVERYTHING
- Copy all documents (*I know this is a bitch but DO IT*)

Check out the APP Hello Mojo: Divorce Administrator. It is a great way to keep everything all in one private place on your phone.

 **Create a checklist** and make sure you have all of these covered and copied:

- Will
- POA
- HCP
- Mortgage
- Title
- Deed
- Insurance: Home, Car, Health and Life
- Bank Accounts
- Investments
- Retirement Accounts
- Do you need a Safety Deposit Box? Do you know where the key is?
- Is there cash in the house?
- Do you know where your valuable art, jewelry, furnishings are?
- Do you have receipts and documentation (photographs) of everything?

Other important documents to have made **copies and pictures** of are:
- Birth Certificates
- Driver's license
- Passports (Children's too)
- Social security cards

This step can take some time…**so get started and get it done!!!**

Lesson Two
Gathering Evidence

While you're at it…it's never a bad idea to gather the facts (aka evidence). Even if you're living in a "no-fault" state, collecting tangible evidence is essential. You may never need it …but you will be happy if you ever do.

1. **Find and keep** papers, photos, email, text messages, voice mail, video, audio, schedules, wrappers, prescriptions, bills, receipts, hotel reservations, flight reservations and gifts. Even if you don't think you need a copy, receipt, proof of purchase…YOU DO. IF you can't find or locate or even worse, DO NOT have access to documentation of receipts, TAKE PICTURES and put them in a secure file on your laptop or phone.

2. IF you are concerned about secrecy, hidden money, missing documents, hard drives that disappear, your phone is missing or your files seem empty, closed bank accounts or tax refunds and insurance claims you are not aware of…. it's time to call in the big guns. Who are the big guns you ask???

3. **Private investigators and Forensic Accountants**. Finding hidden assets is never easy, but it will create a trail to prove that you are not crazy and that your spouse has been secreting funds, real estate, businesses, assets, relationships etc. **Trust your GUT and listen to it**. IF something is telling you to…stop and turn around and open a drawer, answer the phone, look in the trash, check the trunk, ask a stranger, call a random number, check out an address, walk past a location, open a bag, look in the closet…etc. DO IT. This does not mean being paranoid. This does not mean to LOOK for trouble, BUT learn to trust your instincts and keep your eyes and ears open.

- **This means to be smart and savvy.**
- **This means to be wise and mature.**
- **This means to be courageous.**

This **does NOT mean to be stupid or illegal or nosey or disrespectful,** just to be aware and curious about things you may have overlooked before. Have you taken the time to gather the facts (aka evidence)?

Lesson Three
Importance of a Budget

Having a very **clear picture of your finances** is very important. Regardless of how much or how little money you have, you need to know precisely.

Create a **"real and ideal"** budget profile to include:

1. Income and expenses
2. Support needed
3. Marital home maintenance
4. Debt: separate and marital

"Real" is what it is. "Ideal" is what would be ideal if you were on your own and needed more security.

Use Mint or QuickBooks to document your spending habits.

You may also want to consider working with a **Certified Divorce Financial Analyst CDFA to** create a lifestyle analysis for you, which helps determine how much you and your husband spent on average basis month to month and year to year. Having a CDFA analyze your finances gives you an accurate edge ability when you need to clearly demonstrate the financial health of your assets and liabilities when completing your financial statement.

These calculations will be used as a guide to help you develop a budget.

- the day-to-day living expenses incurred during the marriage
- the spending habits of both you and your husband

Don't share with your spouse; keep safe and private.

Consider using an online platform (ie: Mint, Nerd Wallet) for calculating your expenses and budget.

Your budget must be consistent.

- If you are always conservative and frugal.
- If you are extravagant and overly generous.
- It will matter that you show historical spending and saving consistency.

 If you ever do go to court, an inconsistent Financial Statement is a key indicator that it is fabricated.

- Do you know all your living expenses that you incurred during the marriage?
- Do you know your spending habits?
- Do you know your spouse's spending habits?
- Where do you buy gas?
- What do you purchase at coffee shops?
- How much money does your spouse typically spend on gifts? On vacations?
- How often do you eat out?
- Do you choose the least expensive item on the menu? The most?

Have a Certified Divorce Financial Accountant or Planner create a **full lifestyle analysis** to demonstrate financial needs and future goals clearly. It's time to **create a spreadsheet or buy a budget planner journal**. But do it NOW. You will never regret having a clear picture of your finances.

Next, we will dig deep into Lawyer Speak, so it doesn't feel like Greek anymore.

LESSON FOUR
LAWYER SPEAK

It's time to dig into a few Lawyer speak topics. One of the common tactics that are taken by attorneys in difficult litigated divorces is the tactic of "**conflicting out.**"

Because attorneys are prohibited to work with a client who is already familiar with the case and have met the other party, it is common for ONE party will run around and meet with and speak to as many attorneys within a predictable and reasonable driving distance. This prevents their spouse from having the ability to speak to, consult with or hire them.

This is called Conflicting Out. It is not unusual for all the TOP lawyers to meet with many potential clients due to this tactic.

It is also **common for spouses to attempt to HIDE funds** to prevent their spouse from claiming or having access to them.

Common places spouses hide money:

- Transferring assets from joint to individual accounts
- Transferring assets to a friend or family member
- Setting up a life insurance policy
- Overpaying the IRS
- Delaying receipt of payment
- Creating a fake expense
- Bartering for services
- Downplaying the purchase of expensive items
- Lending money to friends or family
- Domestic Trusts
- Offshore accounts

(ATRO- AUTOMATIC TEMPORARY RESTRAINING ORDER)

When one party files, ALL funds are to remain in status quo until the divorce complaint is final. This prevents spending, donating, gifting, selling, transferring, etc. funds during a divorce proceeding.

If one party ignores this, it gets messy and the courts can fine, penalize or find in contempt.

Now it's crucial also to become familiar with common attorney behaviors to pay close attention to during your entire divorce journey... It's common for a spouse to hide their assets, but do you know there are many more techniques up a lawyer's sleeve that you must be aware of.

TYPICAL ATTORNEY TACTICS:

1. Stall and delay tactics. Rescheduling appointments.
2. Exerting pressure to proceed too quickly. Urgency from opposing counsel.
3. Denying access to financial resources. Non-payment, canceling credit cards and closing accounts.
4. Failing to pay court-ordered support or refusing to relinquish assets. Contempt charges do not **always** scare.
5. Falsely claiming their spouse as an abuser **or irresponsible parent**. Hiring a GAL.
6. Using fraud or coercion to obtain credit under their spouse's name and ruin credit by defaulting.

Things will get nasty when one party drags out the proceedings and gets a lawyer involved in the adversarial nature of litigation.

Lawyers will support and stand up for ONE party at all costs.

This does not mean that working with an attorney can't be a positive experience…but be alert.

Time costs money and delaying and dragging procedures out damages relationships.

Be aware that delays are common is all legal proceedings but in family law stall tactics can be used to break down the other sides confidence, build frustration, waste money, express passive aggression and demonstrate authority and control.

You can **download the list of questions you need to ask an attorney** (and other expert professionals when you interview them) from the resources in the Better Divorce Academy website. It is important that you choose an attorney with the correct demeanor to match your goals and your own personality.

Casey Shevin is my contributing attorney that addresses these issues in two bonus modules.

Don't you feel much more prepared to interview an attorney now?

Lesson Five
How to choose your Advocates

You may ask…why do I need advocates?

You may need testimonials. You may need character references. You may need referrals. You may need backup support.

If you have long standing personal and professional relationships with people you work with regularly who can speak on your behalf, such as:

- Realtor
- Mortgage Broker
- Financial Advisor
- Accountant
- Business evaluator
- Private investigator
- Therapist
- Coach
- Children's Teachers or Coaches
- Neighbor
- Community Organizer
- Boss or Co-worker
- Student

It's time to consider who knows you best based on past relationships and business practices:

- Who is trustworthy?
- Who is well-spoken?
- Who is honest?

- Who is experienced in the law?
- Who knows you best?
- Who has always stood by you unconditionally?

If you have a short list, consider yourself lucky. The length of the list is NOT what matters. It is the depth of the list that does.

Family and Friends are not usually the ones to consider as strong advocates.

 It's time to get out your journal and start creating a list of people who you believe will be your best advocates!! You got this!!

LESSON SIX
PLANNERS, CALENDARS AND JOURNALS!

If you are a messy Marvin…
If you are a scatterbrain…
If you are a hoarder and can't seem to find anything…
Now is the time to change all that.

It's time to be organized.
It's time to be thorough.
Everything in its place and a place for everything.

Divorce is a time to get your house in order.
Divorce is a time to simplify.
Divorce is a time to streamline.
Divorce is a time to know what you have, need and want.

And it's a time to know where everything is and maintain control of your life through organization. You can buy separate ones to use throughout the journey or all-in-one.

- Be topic-oriented
- Accordion file for all records and hard copy docs:
- Digital files (downloads)
- Household paperwork
- Email documents
- Online documents

What is the difference between a planner, a calendar, a contact list, a to-do list, and a journal?
Do I have to have them all? I suggest you do.

- A planner is for long term goals
- A calendar is to make and keep track of appointments
- A contact list is to have quick access to phone numbers, emails and addresses
- A journal is a private place to record your emotions, thoughts and feelings and process them as they arise
- A to-do list is essential for keeping track of priorities and in the moment essential tasks
- An accordion file is necessary for organizing the sizeable overwhelming amount of paperwork you will need at a moment's notice.
- Digital apps are also good options to consider

Are you beginning to see the importance of having everything in its place and a place for everything?

Look at how much clarity you have gained from knowing each step to take in getting organized and prepared.

REVIEW
PREP YOUR STEPS

LET'S RECAP …

1. Gather the facts and make copies of everything. **When in doubt, collect and copy it.**
2. When facts are missing… seek them out and don't be afraid to ask professionals for help.
3. You must learn where the money is and where it goes.
4. What are the two tactics lawyers use that you believe would be the most difficult for you?
5. Define your best advocate.
6. Why you need a planner, calendar and journal?

Dig deep to determine who your number one advocate is?

This answer might surprise you.

How can you keep track of everything if you don't have a system?

It's time to get ready for the long haul. Now is the time to start taking care of you.

If you don't do it …who will??? What are you waiting for? Now is the time to prioritize you and your wellbeing.

4

YOU ONLY HAVE YOU TO TAKE CARE OF YOU

SELF CARE IS A DISCIPLINE

You may not think you are ready to proceed if you are falling apart physically, mentally, emotionally and

financially. It's not the time to fall apart and question all the work you have done to get yourself to this point of clarity and conviction.

Let's get serious now about how difficult it is to get through the entire divorce process if you are not carving out time to practice the art of self-care.

It's time to begin to take care of yourself!

It sounds like one more thing to put on your plate, but it's not one more thing... it's the most important thing.

If you fall apart, get sick or even worse come down with a disease (not uncommon after divorce) you are not going to be able to take care of your children or yourself.

Even in the most cordial of divorces where both parties agree about child custody, child support, spousal support and division of marital assets, it is a difficult time filled with paperwork, decisions and deep emotions.

We will address practical ways to manage stress regardless of the situation you are in, or one that you perceive lies ahead.

It's also imperative to see clearly how over-communicating with family and friends can destroy your confidence and add a bit of unwanted drama.

During times of conflict and stress, you will need to pull from your self-care toolbox to nurture your mind, body and soul.

And finally, you will see how sparking your curiosity and hope to create a better future that you and your family desire and deserve is the reason you are embarking on this life-changing decision.

Can you see how you shouldn't overlook the discipline of self-care? If you don't take care of yourself who will?

LET THE WELLNESS JOURNEY BEGIN

Now is the time to get a physical. Do not put this off! The thought of divorce and the divorce itself is trauma. Your body will begin to wear down and show signs of stress as the effects of trauma set in.

Do not delay attending to your health. If you have a PCP, go and get a physical as soon as you can. Get a baseline now to know if you are off-balance physically or using negative coping methods to the detriment of your health.

TOP SIGNS YOUR HEALTH IS SUFFERING AND AT RISK:

- Insomnia (a sign of anxiety)
- Weakened immune system (higher risk for illness and disease)
- Metabolic syndrome (high blood pressure, high blood sugar and intra-abdominal pressure around the waist are more prone to depression)
- Heart disease (20% higher risk)
- Weight gain (using food for comfort)
- Loss of fitness gains (being consumed with the divorce leads to you stopping exercising or backsliding in fitness goals)
- Mobility problems (tight joints, tired, unmotivated, weakened muscles)
- Mood disorders (susceptible to hormonal factors that can influence the brain chemicals that regulate mood)

This is not an exhaustive list, but you can see the domino effect begin! Divorce can ruin your health.

It's time to consider where you are and stay on top of it. The time to take care of you is NOW. You will need to continue to make it a priority. You and your children need you to be on top of your health… not to mention theirs. We will address that in a later chapter. If you are depressed, seeking the help of a psychologist or psychiatrist (if medication is needed) may be the best route.

They go by many names: Therapist, Counselor, Clinician: all trying to address the root cause of an issue. **There is no shame in seeking a therapist to address physical and mental health concerns.** They will not go away because you want them to go away. Pain and suffering are signs that something is not working and change needs to occur.

Example: If every time you go in the sun you get a sunburn, but you never wear sunscreen, a hat and glasses or better yet, stay out of the sun…you will continue to get a sunburn. Eventually, you will get sun damage and blisters, fever, peeling skin and scars. If you ignore the issue for a long enough time, chances are you will get skin cancer. It's the same with an ailment, pains and symptoms.

The same things happen with your heart and our soul. We must create lasting changes in our lives that are for our benefit and not a detriment. The key here is to know what is not serving you, what is not working and what is harming you.

I am not against pharmaceuticals for mental health when necessary, but many people have success merging traditional and natural medicine. The trouble with getting locked into pharmaceuticals is the waterfall effect. One may lead to another and another and another. Each one has a very long list of scary side effects. Almost all list death as a risk. I don't know about you, but for medication, death is not a risk I am interested in.

I was first prescribed Amitriptyline for anxiety then muscle relaxants for tension and pain, Clonopin, for what I don't even know…but they helped me sleep and I was under the understanding that my doctors always knew best.

How can I argue with or ignore their expert medical advice? **They are the experts…right? They must know what is best for me!**

My anxiety lessened, but so did my memory. I couldn't remember a damn thing. Now that was convenient in a few cases, but it was scary, and I had to hide the fact that I didn't remember something important that had happened or something that I said. I slowly saw the light again when I remembered how helpful my chiropractor had been to me with healing knee, hip and back pain from teaching dance for 25 years.

I made an appointment with my chiropractor, but this time to heal my broken heart, as well as my aching muscles and painful joints. My neurological system was completely out of balance and functioning on a minimal baseline. My immune system was drained, and I was unable to fight off anything. My skin broke out in a nasty red itchy rash, I woke up with Tinnitus (ringing in the ears), showed signs of food allergies and I was exhausted all the time. Within a few spinal adjustments, nutritional supplements and mindful exercise, my symptoms dissipated and ultimately disappeared. I have been drug-free since 2015.

With his recommendation, I found an osteopath as my PCP and functional integrative OB/GYN MD who was able to help me get my hormones back on track. I slowly integrated the recommendations from my chiropractor, osteopath, functional OB/GYN and felt much better.

Other Complementary and Alternative Medicines (CAM) to consider that I have tried that may also help you heal.

- Acupuncture
- Affirmations
- Art, Music and Dance Therapy
- Ayurveda
- Biofeedback
- Body Movement Therapy
- Chinese or Oriental Medicine
- Craniosacral Therapy
- Electromagnetic Therapy
- EMDR
- Herbology
- Homeopathy
- Hypnosis
- Massage
- Mind/Meditation
- Naturopathy
- Nutrition/diet
- Qigong
- Reiki
- Tai Chi
- Tapping
- Visualization and Guided Imagery
- Yoga

Not all methods are suited to all people. It's your job to read, research, ask questions and try a few of them out.

There is no time like NOW to practice the ART of extreme self-care. I owe a lot to Cheryl Richardson and her books *Take Time for Your Life, Life Makeover and The Art of Extreme Self-Care*. Reading Cheryl's books woke me up to the fact that I was the last on my list of people I took care of and prioritized. Just the title of her books woke me up.

I attended one of Cheryl's workshops in Boston and created a "Life Makeover" group with my dear friend Mary Kay Duffy because I knew I needed support and accountability. Making any change in your life is never easy, particularly in times of stress and trauma.

Now it's time to look at what you do to waste time and deplete your energy. Extreme self-care is the opposite of time wasters!

Just like the flight attendants instruct us when we get on a plane, you must put on your own oxygen mask first. If you don't put your mask on…no one else will do it for you.

LESSON TWO
MANAGING STRESS

How do you manage your stress? It's not easy to manage stress when you are going through very stressful times. If you are not managing your emotions, you will have LESS success separating from the legal part of divorce. Keeping a stiff upper lip and going it alone will only get you into a deeper state of fear. The attempt to make it appear as though nothing is wrong will not last long before the internal effects of divorce slowly begin to cause all kinds of signs and symptoms of stress.

It's very common to catch a cold, get the flu, come down with a rash, an allergy, a stomach upset, inflammation, a new ailment, a disease or even worse a serious illness. Feelings of "falling apart" and not functioning normally are a sign something is wrong. You must process your emotions and release negativity.

With the spread of COVID-19, it's even more important to be mindful of your wellbeing and health. Take your time to truly take care of yourself. When the body and mind are stressed, the immune system's ability to fight off antigens reduces. The stress hormone corticosteroid suppresses the effectiveness of the immune system. Anxiety causes the release of stress hormones throughout the body and can weaken your immune response.

Grab your journal and create a list of the physical symptoms you are experiencing and the health goals you have. After you get those emotions off your chest, it's time to consider some of the reasons and tactics that may add stress to the experience of divorce.

Things NOT TO DO. (these will add stress to your life and your spouses.)

Here are seventeen distasteful and frequently provoking maneuvers employed by both men and women during the divorce process that add extreme stress.

1. Rejecting or delaying a raise at work to reduce (or avoid paying) alimony or child support payments: some people quit their jobs rather than pay their partners any money.

2. Hiding assets or money from your spouse: you see this one a lot with people who have their own businesses—particularly cash businesses.

3. While plotting a divorce, you secure money from your partner and hide it in a separate account.

4. Raiding the safe deposit box: who wins the race to the family jewelry?

5. Using the legal system to bankrupt your mate. The judicial system needs to do a better job setting limits with these manipulative characters.

6. Allowing your attorney to slander your spouse needlessly. Some lawyers can get out of control and it's your job to stop them.

7. Agreeing to an amicable divorce and, in turn, hiring the meanest lawyer around. Don't you love those spouses who say, "everything is going to go smoothly," and then proceed to bring a bazooka to a knife fight?

8. Teaming up with your lover to plot a divorce from your spouse. There's nothing like actively enlisting someone to help you destroy your own family.

9. Telling your children that your marriage is over before informing your spouse. This maneuver can place an enormous burden on your kids.

10. Forcing your children to accept your lover (or any new partner) before they've had time to process the divorce emotionally. This one is especially self-serving.

11. Consistently ridiculing your estranged spouse in front of your children. Creating loyalty conflicts won't serve your children well.

12. Making up slanderous stories about your partner to alienate

him or her from your mutual friends. Friends don't usually appreciate manipulation.

13. Dumping your partner when he or she is at a low point emotionally (lost job, hospitalized). Some people like to make a statement.

14. Dumping your partner during a time of celebration (anniversary, giving birth). Some partners insist on sadistically stealing your joy.

15. Divorcing your spouse for his or her best friend. Frequently people seem more upset by the friend's betrayal.

16. Destroying or stealing your partner's property during the divorce process. Cars and clothes are often victims, but the particularly nasty types usually destroy something they know their partner will miss.

17. Locking your partner out of the family house even though he/she isn't a threat to you. If no abuse is involved, this is usually a needless power maneuver to escalate the divorce battle.

I do not bring up these tactics to scare you or give you suggestions… I bring them up to wake you up.

Step back, step aside and allow yourself some healthy downtime.

If you are experiencing any of these, get some help with your stress. If you are causing any of these stressors…please stop. You are only damaging yourself and your children. You may be feeling extreme pressure from time to time. Do your very best to remain calm. Keep it together. Dig into your toolbox for ways you can handle stress. Falling apart is a way of peeling away the old to let in the new.

Notice your ability to manage stress, criticism and negativity.

Ask yourself what your touchpoints are.

Notice your triggers. Just notice and don't judge. Tears and anger are okay, but don't get caught off guard if your spouse tries to present you in a negative light.

It's time to grab your journal.

 ## Journal: How are you going to react?

Can you witness your emotions without overreacting and adding fuel to the fire?

Consider and journal a typical situation, how you may react and how you would prefer to respond.

Commonly, a spouse will claim you are falling apart and state that you are not be able to handle stress.

This accusation could be used against you in mediation or court. It is time to be strong, calm, well and vibrant.

It is time to create a plan for stressful situations that is in your best interests.

1. How can you best do that?
2. What is it that allows you to deal with stress successfully in the past?
3. What tools do you have?
4. What examples do you have?
5. How have you best-handled stress in the past?

Think of the wellbeing of yourself and your children. As cruel as it is …you will be judged for overreacting, underreacting, etc.

Remember, other people don't care about you...they only care about themselves. It sounds harsh, but it's the cold, hard truth. Be the role model you wish to be for your children.

 **Journal: What legacy of composure and grace do you want to leave behind?**

Children model what they see, hear and experience!

"Be the change you wish to see in the world."

Gandhi

In other words...how can you take the high road without throwing in the towel?

NOTES

Lesson Three
Communicating with Family and Friends

Next, we deal with the challenge of how to communicate with family and friends. They have been your tribe and your community. They have been who you turned to in times of need before…so why would you treat them any differently?

It's important to remember that your friends and family are human too.

They will come to your divorce with their own feelings, ideas and agendas. Some may genuinely want what is the very best for you, BUT many will not. They will take sides, and they will pass judgment. They will act foolishly, they will be sad, they will be angry, they will be human too.

Here is your new mantra.
"Go slow: bite sized simple communication."

Gossip is common: expect it! Less is Best. Keep your tribe tight.

Three reasons you shouldn't listen to divorce advice from family and friends:

1. **Every divorce is unique.** What worked for your aunt, cousin or friend has little to do with you.
2. **A little knowledge can be a dangerous thing.**
3. **You can find the professional help you need.** They will be experienced, confidential and objective.

Be judicious when discussing your divorce with family and friends: keep in mind that EVERY type of electronic communication has the potential to leave a digital trail (can and will be used against you). Assume it WILL be used against you to try to prove your spouse's case against your parenting, your buying habits, your behavior and your choice of friends.

Keep in mind: according to the AAML American Academy of Matrimonial Lawyers: 92% of divorce cases using evidence from iPhones, androids, smartphones! It is not a joke. Stay off anything digital as MUCH AS possible.

Can you see how being more aware of how to communicate with friends and family will help you?

So many of my clients fall into this trap of texting wars, email wars and social media wars!

WARNING made. Now it's time to start breaking down the steps to take care of you. I know you are ready for that!!

CARING FOR YOUR MIND AND BODY

Before we dig into how to care for yourself, I'd like you to reflect a bit.

 **How do you step back and care for yourself when you are experiencing so much stress and overwhelm?**

Can you think of a time when you were in a stressful situation and you managed to handle it well?

- What was the situation?
- How did you manage it?
- How did it make you feel?
- What was the outcome of your ability to handle it?

Some of the best ways to relax your mind (to stop it from racing) are:

- Meditation (be still and observe the breath)
- Reading (something inspirational and motivational)
- Listening to music (soothing and uplifting)
- Walk in nature (nature brings us back to a place of grounding, simplicity and self-care)
- Move your body (movement releases endorphins, sweat releases toxins, physical wellness correlates to mental strength)
- Create a regular fitness routine 3 times a week (mix it up! Different styles, speeds, indoor vs outdoor, location, flexibility, cardiovascular, bone density)

- Try a yoga class! Yoga has the magical combination of ALL of these.

All involve periods of mindfulness, meditation, inspirational readings and affirmations, relaxing and motivational music, Zen-like settings, movement, sweat, health benefits and mental clarity.

You are What you Eat

A healthy, well-balanced diet is the only option. Now it is the time to level-up your diet.

- The key element is to stay away from PROCESSED foods. (aka fast food)
- If it is a plant, eat it...if it comes from a plant (manufacturing plant), don't.
- Try to eat your most substantial meal of the day between 10-2 PM instead of after 7:30 PM.
- Aim for 80% of your plate plant-based

In times of stress, don't try too many NEW foods into your diet. Our bodies are most vulnerable during times of stress in developing food sensitivities. Sensitivities can develop into allergies if you consistently eat the same foods. Balance is the goal.

Fiber is no joke. If you are not eating enough fiber, your digestive system will get blocked or stuck.

Chewing your food adequately is not something we usually take much time to think about. But it has everything to do with taking in all the nutrients in the food you are eating. Allowing the process of digestion to begin with your eyes, nose, ears (seeing the food, smelling the food, hearing the food sizzle while cooking), being prepared and calming down the stress response we have when we rush through the ritual of eating.

Here are a few other factors to consider and evaluate.

- Hydration is so important it deserves its own lesson! When the body is dried out, the skin dries out, the mind is sluggish, the body is tired, and we yawn gasping for oxygen and fuel.
- Drink half your weight in ounces each day
- Consider supplements and vitamins with the guidance of a functional MD or chiropractor.
- Alcohol: Wine is an unregulated and non-labeled food. List all the chemicals and sulfites that are in the wine you drink. If you are going to drink minimally in times of stress, be sure you know what is in it.

Remove toxins from your body. When stress is paramount, the body holds on to toxins and has a difficult time releasing them. I will outline a few suggestions and techniques of ways to expedite the body's ability to release stored toxins that can promote illness and disease.

- Dry skin brushing towards the heart (dry brush not the same as a loofah)
- Tongue scraping (use back of a spoon if you don't want to buy a tongue scraper)
- Oil pulling (use oil specifically for oil pulling OR pure organic coconut oil)
- Neti Pot (available on Chopra or whole foods, ceramic is best)
- Nasya Oil (organic is best…essential if you live in high altitudes or dry climates)
- Oil skin (lotion is loaded with dimethicone and other chemicals)

Check the Environmental Working Group website to check for toxicity.

- Skincare (more than 7000 chemicals and toxins unregulated by US government)

- Fragrance (highly toxic)
- Makeup (endocrine disruptors)
- Haircare (scalp is a pure pathway to the brain and neurological system)
- Nail polish (most polish is poison and direct cuticle access)

And in your home:

- Start with under the sink. What's there? Is it toxic? Has it expired? Is it still healthy to use?
- Consider your bathroom and kitchen products!! (cleaners, detergents, toiletries etc.)
- The amount of toxins, chemicals, carcinogens is scary!! What are you using?
- 70% Isopropyl alcohol is good for killing viruses and bacteria on surfaces.

I know this online course is not centered around changing our wellness products. I do wish to impress upon you the need to open your eyes as to the number of toxins in your home, your office, your work environment, your schools, etc. Stay aware and make small but meaningful choices and smart decisions.

Avoid slipping into negative habits. Build your awareness of your negative patterns and habits slipping under our radar. If you are only eating comfort food, not eating enough, staying up late, not wanting to work out, not being able to sleep, etc. IT IS TIME TO address these issues NOW.

Stress and illness go hand and hand. "I"llness = I "We"llness = We... meaning it's a good thing to ask for help.

In times of stress don't go it alone.

LESSON FIVE
NURTURING YOUR SOUL

How do you nurture our soul in times of extreme stress?

Feeding your soul with meditation and tuning into your intuitive skills is simple and effective.

That is not to say it is easy to do. It takes some practice and acceptance that your mind will wander, and you may become distracted and want to quit. Give it some time and just like brushing your teeth, it will become a habit.

Let's start by getting down to basics with meditation. Meditation reminds you to pay attention to the fundamentals.

I have created a list of suggestions for you to consider.

CREATE A SPACE
Meditating at home is convenient, so design an area where you can sit in comfort. Clear away any clutter. Sweep and dust to freshen the air. Set out candles, incense, and peaceful images.

CHECK YOUR POSTURE
Scan your body for any signs of tension. Unclench your jaw and lower your shoulders. Straighten your back to help you stay alert.

FOLLOW YOUR BREATH
Inhale deeply and let the flow of oxygen rise, expanding your abdomen and chest. Spend an equal amount of time gently exhaling. Enjoy the peaceful feeling as you notice your torso lift and fall.

OBSERVE YOUR THOUGHTS

Allow your thoughts to come and go without trying to control them. Acknowledge what's on your mind, and let it pass just as you would observe a car passing by or a cloud blowing by in the wind.

LET GO OF JUDGEMENTS

Accept your feelings and experiences. Adopt an attitude of curiosity without labeling things as being good or bad. Thoughts are just thoughts. They lose their power when you let them go.

CULTIVATE GRATITUDE

Deepen your sense of connection by remembering the kindness that you receive from others. Picture the friendly barista who wished you a good morning or the coworker who gives you constructive feedback. Give thanks for your neighbors, family and friends.

ENCOURAGE GENEROSITY

Recognize that happiness and fulfillment come from giving. Look for ways to share your wisdom and resources.

DEVELOP COMPASSION

Conflicts are unavoidable, but they can enhance relationships when you work towards resolving them. Put yourself in someone else's shoes by thinking about what they're trying to accomplish instead of focusing on how they irritate you. You may discover compromises that will satisfy you both.

CLARIFY YOUR PURPOSE

Meditation can be secular or part of your faith tradition. Maybe you want to relax after a day at the office or looking after your kids. Maybe you want to deepen your spiritual insights.

SEEK SUPPORT

While you can meditate on your own, reaching out to others is likely to help you make more progress. If you're a beginner, find a class or browse for instructions online. If you have years of experience, look for a partner or group to share your practice.

PROCEED GRADUALLY

Even a few minutes of mindfulness practice can transform your day. Listen to your inner voice and experiment to find what brings you peace.

- Meditate as consistently as you eat.
- Massage is your next step to releasing tension and stuck energy in the physical body. Massage schools need a body to practice on if money is tight.
- Use those moments sitting at a red light, waiting in line at the grocery store, in the doctor's office or for the kids to get off the bus to sit in silence and watch the flow of your breath.
- Look around your environment and see how your environment makes you feel.
- If your environment is cluttered, if your office is cluttered, chances are good that so is your mind!
- Learn to practice the magical art of tidying up. Let to let go with grace.

IF you haven't heard of Marie Kondo…check out her work. No need to hold on to anything that does not "**SPARK JOY**" and serve a purpose, or ultimately BOTH.

Lightening your physical load frees up space and energy to unveil your emotions and values as well as the thoughts in your mind.

Consider the practice of **YOGA NIDRA**. Yoga Nidra, by definition, is the most profound state of rest without being asleep.

Yoga Nidra walks you through the different states of brain waves.

- GAMMA (40-80 CSP Cycles Per Second) Superconscious. Highly attentive, high-level information processing, higher mental activity and organization of information. If too much it can lead to anxiety, high alert, stress

- BETA (13-39) Conscious. Fully awake and alert. (aka "ordinary reality.")
- ALPHA (8-13) Subconscious. Deeply relaxed. Light hypnosis, meditation, biofeedback, daydreaming, listening to music, matching a movie
- THETA (4-8) Superconscious...drowsy, tranquil, unconscious, light sleep, shamanic journeying, 5th dimension, non-ordinary reality
- DELTA (.5-4) Dream State...Deeply unconscious, sleep, astral travel, dreaming

Yoga Nidra is a unique marriage of science and spirit, combining alert awareness and most profound relaxation. It takes your brain to the alpha state and, eventually, the deeper theta wave state. Here, without effort or strain, you tap into your source of intuition, creativity, health and abundance.

Yoga Nidra is practiced in a comfortable lying down position. You are guided through a series of breathing exercises and simple instructions. Some of these include visual imagery or a scan of the body, which occupies the mind and prevents it from becoming involved in the usual mind-chatter that absorbs our ordinary consciousness.

Within a short time, you become submerged in the alpha state, where brain rhythms drop into the silent space within.

Once your body is relaxed and your mind is calm, all energies are focused on the "Third Eye", the inner sanctuary located between the eyebrows. Here you are simultaneously able to access both the logical left brain and the intuitive, insightful right brain. This naturally and effortlessly brings integration, where you experience deep relaxation yet remain aware and conscious.

Modern science now confirms what yogis discovered thousands of years ago: that focusing on the Third Eye reactivates hormones located in the pineal gland in the center of the brain.

Studies confirm that the pineal gland hormone, melatonin, is a powerful agent in helping prevent illness, retard premature aging, reduce stress, induce more restful sleep, boost the immune system, and promote healing.

Research has proven the benefits of this technique on lowering stress and promoting overall health.

Yoga Nidra allows you to drop into a sleep-like state with relaxed brainwave activity. Slow alpha waves, and even slower theta waves, produce deep relaxation and are the entry points to the subconscious.

In this state, you can make a conscious crossover from the logical left brain to the intuitive right brain, connected to the field of conscious intelligence, where the intention is carried out spontaneously and effortlessly.

One purpose of yoga and Yoga Nidra is to initiate the integrative process that balances the sympathetic and parasympathetic nervous systems, and the left and right brain.

Yoga Nidra saved me when I was going through my divorce. I practiced it at least once a day, usually in the afternoon, for 10-15 minutes under the guidance of my teacher Rod Stryker's expert instruction.

There are MANY online versions of Yoga Nidra. Rod Stryker's practice is in the APP "Sanctuary".

Let's recap here:

- Do your very best to unplug from your day (Email, TV, Social Media, etc.) by 9:00 PM.
- Do not eat after 7:30 PM
- Take a bath
- Listen to relaxing music
- Sip Herbal Tea
- Journal

- Prepare for your day
- Set an intention for your sleep
- Fall asleep by 10:30 PM
- Awaken by 6:30 AM

Divorce isn't just about your finances.

You have no choice but to care for the body, mind and spirit given to you.

LESSON SIX
BE CREATIVE WITH YOUR FUTURE

Lesson six takes us deeper into the path of exploring and managing self-care during the divorce process. And don't think for a minute that after this stressful time in your life is complete, you can forget all that you have learned…in fact, you won't want to.

Let's be creative with your future.

The future seems impossible.
The future seems so far away.
The future seems miserable.

How can you get creative with your future if you can't get through today?

First, let's visualize …what do you want? What is your goal? What are you trying to bring into your life?

Dare bravely…go out on a limb and describe the life you believe you deserve, and your family deserves. The more you decide what you want and visualize it, the more your brain and soul knows it to be true.

The Law of Attraction gets a lot of press. If you think and feel and see negativity, doubt and fear, the more you attract it. And the SAME goes for positivity.

 I want you to stop and close your eyes and **SEE the results you want**, actually, *see* the results of this divorce coming alive.

1. What did you agree to?
2. What did you create?
3. What did you give and what did you get?
4. Where are you living?
5. What are you doing for work?
6. How are you serving?
7. Who are you serving?
8. How are you thriving?
9. How are your children thriving?

The more you do that …2/3 times a day, the better.

When negative thoughts and actions trigger you, you can disrupt your negative thinking. You must learn to be a strong advocate for yourself. The universe is calling you to be a strong advocate for yourself and to design the results you desire and deserve for you and your family.

Internalize …your thoughts become a part of who you are …part of your being. Your thoughts become a part of your DNA.

And finally, Realize. You need to believe you can get what you believe you deserve.

 **Grab your journal and let's walk through these questions together.**

- What brought you joy in the past?
- What do you want your life to look like in the future?
- How do you view change?

- How can you simplify your life to allow yourself to feel calm, centered and prepared for each day?
- Who do you want to be in the future?
- How do you want to look back at this experience ten years from now?

And then:

1. Can you see how you have more control over your future than you thought you did?
2. Can you see how having a clear sight and vision of your future is helpful?
3. How do you feel now that you can visualize, internalize and realize the future you desire is real?

REVIEW
NOW IS THE TIME FOR SELF CARE

Phew!! That was a lot of self-study and exploration.

I am so proud of you for opening yourself up to so much possibility and self-care and self-love. Now is the time for self-care! Self-care is always important, but while going through a divorce, it is especially important. There is a reason that flight attendants tell us to put our oxygen mask on first before assisting our children.

- When you are not well, how can you possibly help anyone else?
- What are a few simple ways you can integrate extreme self-care?
- How can you find support that is a good and empowering fit?
- How do you currently deal with unmanaged stress… how is it harming you?

 **What changes can you make to manage your stress levels?**

For example:
- Are you going to bed earlier?
- Stepping back from toxic family members?
- Difficult and judgmental friends?
- Taking a walk in nature instead of running to the refrigerator?

Name three changes you're ready to implement.

Your health and wellness should be priority #1.
So, what are you waiting for?
What do you desire for your future?

Be sure to describe it in detail in your journal.

5

GET FAMILIAR WITH THE PROCESS

DON'T GO IT ALONE

It's time to get familiar with the divorce process. It's time to learn who the players are.

You need to build your "A-Team."

I recall the TV show "The A-Team" back in the 1980s. The A-Team was an American action-adventure television series that ran on NBC from 1983 to 1987 about former members of a fictitious United States Army Special Forces unit. The members, after being court-martialed „for a crime they didn't commit," escaped from military prison and, while still on the run, worked as soldiers of fortune. They were **the best of the best** and there seemed to be nothing they couldn't do. This is the mindset and team you need to have to support YOU.

I needed an **A-Team** …but I didn't have one.

What a mistake that was!

I used my lawyer as a therapist, and it cost a bloody fortune!

When I wrote 3-page emails to my attorney, I overlooked that I was paying him to read them, research my questions, answer them, forward them to others, etc. I honestly had no idea that he was charging me to read an email!

When I did figure that out, I had become so accustomed to reaching out to him for any little concern, every little question and confirm my wishes that I kept doing it regardless of the cost. I tried to keep it to a minimum, but it was a habit and he was my lifeline to communication, answers and an end in sight.

I have come to learn that in the last few years, some attorneys and firms charge in 6-10-minute intervals. If their hourly rate is $500 an hour (not unusual) and you send them an email for even the simplest of questions requiring a yes or no, it could cost you as much as $75 just to get a quick yes or no email response. **If your attorney's rate is $500 an hour…that is $8.33 per MINUTE!**

Emails and phone calls are just the tip of the iceberg. You will be billed for literally EVERYTHING and ANYTHING that concerns your case. It's all about the Benjamin's…according to some 90's rap song. Of course, he had no reason to stop all those billable hours.

After the first few months of bills arrived in my mailbox with a blow by blow list of all "billable" activities, communication, transactions, writing etc., I kept communication to only what was necessary. At least I tried, but it didn't take long for my retainer to be gone!! Attorneys cost a fortune. It's easy to forget they charge by the minute. **Bear in mind. Most attorneys are not in any rush to finalize your divorce.**

However, if you don't hire **and work with** an attorney, it could be a disaster waiting to happen when you're not protected by understanding your legal rights. It could mean your spouse controls the process through their attorney. They may slow things down or hastening things in a way that may not work for your timetable.

Your attorney looks after your best interests as your advocate. It is one of the things they learn in law school. How to be a voracious advocate for their client. This can be good or bad, but you can see how the very nature of this dynamic sets up a naturally adversarial environment for both parties. Both attorneys are committed to seeing this through to the end for the benefit of THEIR client…not the benefit of the family as a whole.

Family law attorneys are trained to look out for the legal rights of ONE party...so keep in mind it is adversarial by nature.

Everyone is fighting to win-win-win.

The bottom line is that I advise you not to go it alone. There are options and we'll go through them.

There are three parts to creating your A-Team.

You will need three pillars of support:

1. **Family and Friends (advocates)**
2. **Professionals**
3. **Self: You need to bring your A-game too**

In this chapter, you will learn the importance of each leg you need to stand on, family and friends (advocates), professionals and yourself. Each pillar is equally important. Without one, it's like a tripod with only two legs. It just won't hold up.

You need to know the law... for your protection. Consulting with at least three attorneys to fact-find does not mean you need to hire one on a retainer basis.

Mediation versus litigation benefits you by being a cheaper, alternative dispute resolution.

The role of a mediator is to be a neutral party that facilitates communication between divorcing spouses looking to iron out the division of marital assets, the parenting plan, and the spousal and/or child support.

The evidence I've seen is that reaching a parenting plan and custodial agreement is better in the hands of the parents than a judge...unless it's for the safety and well-being of the children. You will learn the importance of reaching a custodial agreement before you head to a lawyer or judge. It's not always possible, but it's always best. If there's an impasse, parties still have the right to go to court.

Let's dig into the **roles of all the professionals** you could use in your divorce. The idea of delegating responsibility to anyone. Without thought, that is "in charge" of your future and the future of your children is not wise. It is advisable in some cases and inadvisable in others.

Here are some key questions to ask before deciding which process is best for you.
Note the answers in your journal.

- How will your spouse deal with the prospect of divorce after the initial emotional impact has diminished? Will they be a bully, a "my way or the highway" negotiator, or will they try to be fair and listen to all sides before deciding?
- How do you want to look back and remember how you were during the divorce process? Do you want to be angry and emotional or as someone who is credible and an excellent communicator?
- Are there considerations that are important to you? Such as privacy from public disclosure, or involvement in the decision- making process, or focus on children. Also, participation by both parties, or length of the process, or control of the pace of the process, or emotional impact. Any of these could dictate a preference of process for you?
- Do you want to be a client who partners with your spouse through mediation? Or do you need a buffer, like an attorney between you and your spouse?
- Do you want to be actively involved in the decision-making, or do you want to give the power of decision making over

to your attorney and let him or her loose to get a "win" for your side?

- How do you want to model effective behavior to others, your children, your family, or your community?
- How do you envision redefining the relationship with your spouse after the divorce is over? Will you be co-parents, former spouses now still loyal to both of your families, or will you cut all ties with his family and the communities you shared?
- What are you most afraid of during the divorce process? How would you expect the attorney to engage with you in this?
- What kind of relationship do you want to have with your attorney?
- What is important to you in any business relationship? Do you want top-notch service, or do you want options as to how you can use their services more cost-effectively? Do you want to be a partner with that person or just have them lead the process?

You can see how important it is to know the difference and always oversee your future. It's time to know the cast of characters and who you will on your team.

LESSON ONE
KNOW THE LAW.

I am not an attorney. I am a mediator and a Certified Divorce Coach and Specialist, and I do know a fair amount about the legal process of divorce. But.... **I do not give legal advice.** The purpose of this lesson is to familiarize you with the process. You must read the laws in your state to become familiar with them.

In the **Better Divorce Academy Course,** there are bonus modules where **Attorney Casey Shevin** will walk you through more of the legal landscape of working with an attorney and learning how to use your attorney efficiently and effectively.

There are five different processes that we will go through, but first, **let's clarify a few legal terms** with which you should be familiar.

1. *Legal separation*: an arrangement by which a couple remain married but live apart; following a court order.
2. *Advantages of legal separation*...allows couples to make financial decisions regarding child support and alimony and live apart without the formality of divorce. It is possible to reconcile easier if issues are resolved.
3. *Uncontested vs. contested.* Uncontested is where both parties agree on all the terms of the divorce and do not need the court to make decisions for them. Contested is when the parties cannot come to terms and require the courts to intervene.
4. *Default:* When one party does not answer the complaint within the required time frame. Sometimes when two parties are in complete agreement with everything, they will ignore the complaint charge to avoid the courts.

5. *Annulment:* An annulment makes a marriage null and void. As if it never happened. Usually in cases of false pretense or very short periods of time.

6. ***Ending Common Law marriage***: aka informal marriage or marriage by habit to live together for a period, be over 18 years of age and of sound mind and body, not married to someone else, they must intend to be married. They present themselves as married to family and friends, take the same name, refer to each other as husband and wife, hold joint bank accounts. Only nine states recognize common law marriage. Common-Law states are 50/50. Equitable distribution states are what the law sees as fair but not necessarily equal.

7. ***Residency*** is considered where you can file for a divorce complaint. Not where you were married or where you have lived but where you pay taxes, vote and own property.

Now it's time to understand entering the process in "good faith."

This means:

1. **You are responsible for filling out your complete financial statement...honesty and completely.**
2. **You are entitled to full disclosure from your spouse.**
3. **You are entitled to an opportunity to tell the judge what your complaint is.**
4. **You are entitled to be treated with respect and fair judgment.**

Now, will that happen? It may and it may not. Do not assume one way or the other. It's always best to not take anything for granted. The trouble with hearsay .... The rule prohibits hearsay (out of court statements offered as proof of that statement) from being admitted as evidence because of the inability of the other party to cross-examine the maker of the statement. "He said this" and "she said that"

.... if there is no evidence or witness it is called hearsay. Therefore, **you need to document everything. When in doubt, take a picture, write it down, get some physical evidence. You just never know.**

In most cases, you cannot "disinherit" your spouse until the divorce is final. You can then change your will, medical directive, living will etc., but not before.

That does not stop many bitter people from trying and doing it anyway.

These laws and explanations are essential to be familiar with. Can you see how important it is to be familiar with the laws in your state and common legal terms you may hear?

Coming up in lesson two, we will consider a deeper dive into the role and responsibilities of an attorney and what it is like working with one.

Lesson Two
Find a Family Law Attorney

How can you find a top-notch attorney and not have to pay CRAZY high fees?

Word of mouth is best…but you must meet a lawyer and ask them questions to get a feel for how they approach divorce. Lawyers are people too and they come in all shapes and sizes, temperaments and specialties.

Referrals are key. If you know a few people who managed to survive divorce well OR you know a few people who had challenging high conflict divorces and managed to come out unscathed…get their number.

Find the top three in your town or area to meet and interview as soon as possible.

How can you ask legal questions and get honest answers and not have to pay a retainer?

Call to make an appointment to interview and slip in your questions. Dress professionally and ask- ask- ask. Asking questions in a meet and greet first meeting is usually complementary or at a reasonable rate for their time.

Download the PDF of what to ask from the Better Divorce Academy website, print and keep it handy when you meet with them.

List of questions to ask Attorneys.

It is very easy to get your questions mixed up when your emotions and fears take over. Stay calm, ask questions and thank them for their time. Try to get as much "legal advice" from them as you can and not commit to any further relationship or retainer. It's crucial to **GO PREPARED** when you interview a lawyer. They cannot give you sound advice if they do not have any current facts.

You will need to bring with you...

- All financial documents, i.e. bank, investments, IRA, etc.
- All income statements i.e. W2, 1099, etc.
- All property documents i.e. title
- All business documents i.e. real estate, LLC ownership
- Any child-related documents i.e. medical, parenting plans
- All assets and debts
- All credit card info
- Anything else you believe to be relevant

WHAT IS MARITAL PROPERTY?

Marital property is a **US**-state-level legal term that refers to property acquired during a marriage. Property that an individual owns before a marriage is considered separate property, as are inheritances or third-party gifts given to an individual during a marriage. Marriage partners may choose to exclude specific property from marital property by signing a "prenuptial" or a "postnuptial" agreement.

Prenuptial is a legal binding document written before a couple is married that irons out who gets what in the event the couple divorces. This can get sticky when it comes to long-term marriages where there are now assets the couple did not think about years beforehand.

Postnuptial is a legal agreement that a couple writes and signs after they are married that describes how assets would be divided in the event of divorce. Both prenuptial and postnuptial agreements have their benefits. If either or both parties have assets they wish to protect or children from a previous marriage they are not unusual and often can save anger, hurt and legal arguments in the event of divorce. Unfortunately they can also cause lack of trust, upset feelings and impede a sense of romance, but if full disclosure is intact and future financial provisions are included, written well and both parties have ample time to consult with an attorney and are in full agreement they are hugely beneficial.

Both can be contested in court.

Some of the details described below won't affect a couple unless they divorce or until one of them dies. But couples need to learn about the different types of marital property so that when they acquire real estate or other property, they know how ownership can be arranged and choose the structure that represents their true intentions.

KEY TAKEAWAYS

1. Marital property refers to property that a couple acquires during their marriage.
2. "Where a couple lives" determines the laws that govern the distribution of marital property in the event of divorce.
3. In common-law property states, property that is acquired by one spouse is considered their sole property unless the title or deed carries both spouses' names.
4. Nine states are community property states, where marital property acquired during the marriage is owned by both spouses equally.

Understanding marital **property**; Marital property includes real estate and other property a couple buys together during their marriage, such as a home or investment property, cars, boats, furniture, or artwork.

Also, bank accounts, pensions, securities, and retirement accounts are also included; even an IRA, which is individually owned by law, is marital property if earned income is contributed to it during marriage.

This legal definition of marital property primarily exists to protect spousal rights.

A couple's permanent legal residence—in either a common law property state or a community property state—determines which laws govern their marital property and how it can be divided if their marriage ends in divorce.

Marital Property: Common Law Property States vs. Community Property States.

Which type of state you live in generally determines what is marital property.

Common Law Property States

Most states are common law property states. The common law system provides that property acquired by one member of a married couple is owned completely and solely by that person. Under this legal framework, if the title or deed to a piece of property is put in the names of both spouses, the property belongs to both spouses.

If both spouses' names are on the title, each owns a one-half interest. If a wife buys a car and puts it only in her name, for example, the car belongs to her only. However, if she buys the car and puts it in both her and her husband's names, the car belongs to both.

Under common-law, when one spouse passes away, their separate property is distributed according to their will—or according to probate, if there is no will in effect.

How this distribution pans out depends on which type of legal ownership the spouse has in any marital property.

If they own property in "joint tenancy with the right of survivorship" or "tenancy by the entirety," the property goes to the surviving spouse.

This right is independent of what the deceased spouses will says.

However, if the property was owned as "tenancy in common," then the property can go to someone other than the surviving spouse, per the deceased spouse's will.

Not all property has a title or deed. In this case, generally, whoever paid for the property or received it as a gift owns it.

Community Property States
Arizona, California, Idaho, Louisiana, Nevada, New Mexico, Texas, Washington, and Wisconsin are all community property states. These nine states follow the rule that all assets acquired during a marriage are considered community property.

Alaska has an "opt-in" community property law that allows such a division of property, providing both parties agree.

Marital property in community property states is owned by both spouses equally. This marital property includes earnings, all property bought with those earnings, and all debts accrued during the marriage.

Couples residing in community property states must account for their community income as well as their separate income if they file separate federal tax returns.

Community property begins at the marriage and ends when the couple physically separates with the intention of not continuing

the marriage. Therefore, any earnings or debts originating after separation are considered separate property.

Marital Property and Divorce

If the couple divorces or obtains a legal separation and the former spouses can't decide how to divide their marital property, a court will decide for them.

Of course, the couple can enter into a prenup agreement before the marriage, explaining how to distribute the marital property upon divorce.

Usually, if the prenup is valid and doesn't violate federal or state laws, it will be followed—even in community property states.

Conflicting out top attorneys: Attorney-Client relationship prevents your spouse from being able to use them. This is also an excellent reason to GO MEET with the top lawyers in your area so your spouse CAN'T use them.

IF you ever decide to go ahead and hire an attorney, there are some important things to remember. Remember the cost of attorney: retainer and billing > keep in mind that every phone call and email is a billable hour.

Ways to afford a divorce:

- Pro Bono
- Public Interest Groups: Legal Services Corp., Catholic Charities, Veterans
- Bar Associations
- Law Schools...contact law school clinics
- Family loans (not the best choice)
- Credit Card (not the best choice)

Going into debt to divorce is common, but not advised.

If divorce has been on your radar for a while, but you have not saved money and put it aside to cover the expenses…it's time to get creative. If you have set money aside…this is a good thing. Don't fret if you haven't! Do everything you can to visit the top attorneys, get the advice of an attorney, gather your facts and figures and hold off on using one.

If and when you are ready to engage in a contract with an attorney, the energy and momentum of divorce will change. Here are a few more professionals you will need to know and how to best use their skills and experience in the laws and processes.

What do a receptionist, paralegal and legal clerk have in common… they are your new FAMILY! You need to be kind and friendly with all of them because they control the process; they don't just prepare legal documents. Do not overlook the importance of forming a relationship with the legal staff in the office of your attorney and other divorce professional's office. They are the bloodline to the security and future of your divorce agreement or settlement.

You can sneak in a question here or there.
You can get a phone call response faster.
You can receive all kinds of hints and tips…" free" if you can manage to establish a positive and solid rapport.

Wow! That was a lot of information. How are you doing so far?

Getting up to speed with the legal profession as a whole is a HUGE benefit. Take a minute to step back and digest the facts about the legal field and how it will affect you.

Next, professionals in the field of divorce that can save you money, help you with the organization and overwhelm, and allow you to have a better divorce experience.

Now that sounds a lot better…doesn't it?!!

NOTES

Lesson Three
Professional Experts and Coaches

Here we are going to cover **Mediators and Coaches**. This one is close to my heart.

These are the professionals that will make all the difference and preserve your money, your mind and your soul. Divorce is hard enough…let's make it easier by feeling heard, seen and respected. Divorce mediation is an alternative to court litigation for resolving disputes that arise as two people separate their lives. A neutral third party called a "mediator" helps the couple to work through the issues of their divorce and reach a mutually agreeable settlement.

The benefits of divorce through mediation may include:

1. **Control: When a couple divorces through a trial, a judge will make the decisions regarding their marital issues.**

2. **Confidentiality: Mediation is a completely confidential process. Litigation is public.**

3. **Speed: Mediation can be a quicker process than other methods of divorce. Less Expensive!!**

BUT here are a few things to consider before you jump on board!

Must-haves for mediation success.

1. BOTH parties must be willing to attend and actively participate in mediation voluntarily.
2. BOTH parties are comfortable and interested in making their own decisions.

3. BOTH parties must be mentally capable of making their own decisions (safe and free of coercion)

4. BOTH parties are willing to be completely transparent and engage in a good-faith negotiation

Because the mediation process is transparent, you and your spouse will both need to be prepared to engage in good-faith negotiation. That means you'll need to reveal and openly disclose all relevant information, whether financial or otherwise, to the mediator and your spouse and ensure that the information is accurate, complete and truthful to the best of your knowledge.

If either party is hiding assets, defrauding the other or not being honest, you will not be able to mediate. High conflict or low conflict, whether only one of you controlled the finances or you both balanced the checkbook, kids or no kids, as long as you and your husband or wife meet the guidelines listed above, you are good candidates to use divorce mediation.

Next, you'll learn about the **most significant benefits of divorce mediation**:

1. Divorce mediation is the most child-focused of all divorce options.

2. Mediation can help you get through your divorce in less time, with less stress and at a lower cost than a lawyer-driven divorce.

3. Mediation enables you to have an amicable divorce.

4. Divorce mediation is the most flexible of the divorce methods, allowing you to control the pace of your divorce and the terms of your settlement.

5. Divorce mediators empower both you and your spouse to create an agreement that meets your unique needs, allowing each of you to get what you want, need and deserve to move forward with your lives.

The finance of mediation:

1. More cost-effective than hiring an attorney (average cost in large cities $78-200K) or doing it yourself (average cost 27-32K) versus mediation (average cost 5-10k) Some mediators charge a flat fee while others charge hourly.
2. Do you have that kind of money to spend on your divorce? Even if you did, do you want to? To start, most divorce lawyers require an initial retainer of between $3,500 and $10,000 per person depending upon the complexity of your case and how well you and your spouse get along. So, before you even negotiate your first point, your divorce will cost $10,000 to $20,000.
3. By the time things wrap up, you could be looking at tens or hundreds of thousands of dollars more to get your divorce. With mediation, both spouses will work with one mediator who is dedicated to helping them both reach a resolution as quickly and efficiently as possible.
4. The total average cost of mediation is between $5,000 and $10,000. And some divorce mediators don't require a retainer. You pay as you go. Or, better yet, you might find a mediator who offers a flat fee so you can know up-front precisely what your mediation will cost from start to finish.

Why is mediation so cost-effective?

First, you're working with one mediator instead of two divorce lawyers. So, you've already cut the number of professionals involved in half.

Second, there's no back and forth between attorneys. All communication is done in real-time, between all parties and out of court. Allowing you to resolve issues faster, thus keeping costs in check.

Finally, because mediation is about problem-solving and agreement building instead of each attorney trying to prove a point and "win" something for their side, solutions are reached much more quickly.

Here are a few other **mediation points to consider**:

1. Less time for case completion equals much lower costs for you.
2. Mediation is empowering and fair ...both parties feel heard and respected
3. Mediation has a higher rate of compliance ...continue to follow the agreement
4. Mediation results in more thorough and practical agreements ...one you can stick to and use
5. Mediation is a more personalized and dignified experience
6. Mediation is more convenient and flexible
7. Mediation can be done virtually online for greater convenience and security
8. Meditation is private and confidential

And to walk down the path of mediation even more, here are more **situations and outcomes that are possible**:

1. How mediation is the most peaceful and child-focused of all divorce options.
2. How mediation can help you get through your divorce in less time, with less stress and at a lower cost than a lawyer-driven divorce.
3. How mediation is the most flexible of the divorce methods, allowing you to control the pace of your divorce and the terms of your settlement.
4. How mediation empowers both you and your spouse to create a fair and thorough agreement that meets your unique needs and the individual needs of your children.
5. Mediation is often court-ordered to settle out of court or recommended by lawyers who realize it can be worked out without using a judge.
6. If spouses agree to disclose and engage, 75% of divorce cases settle faster and cheaper.
7. It allows both parties to be heard and in control of the outcome.

8. 100% confidential as opposed to getting the court involved that is all public
9. Still can land in court if negotiations stall or come to an impasse.
10. You have other options available to you if mediation fails

The responsibilities of a mediator:

Mediators have a responsibility to explain the process to you and your spouse thoroughly. You both should not feel rushed and you both should have ample time to have your questions answered.

During the initial consultation, they will explain an overview of the divorce mediation process – a divorce mediator will explain the entire mediation and divorce process as well as provide a timeline of how divorce in your state works.

Your questions will be answered, and ample time will be devoted to answering your questions. You will need to decide if mediation is right for you based on the facts.

You will hear about process options for divorce in your state to better understand whether mediation is right for your situation. You will need to understand the mediation process. A detailed overview will be provided on what happens at mediation, outside mediation, and after mediation.

You should leave your consultation feeling a sense of relief – Divorce is difficult, but divorce mediation makes it easier. Working with a neutral person (the mediator) can provide both structure and a safe place for productive conversations.

Mediators can be attorneys, but when acting as a mediator, they do not give legal advice.

Mediators can be financial advisors, but when acting as a mediator, they do not give financial advice.

Mediators can be mental health professionals, but when acting as a mediator, they do not diagnose nor treat mental health concerns.

Mediators can be Certified Divorce Coaches, but when acting as a mediator they do not advise, prepare, plan, research, support or the parties.

Mediators are not coaches: They are a neutral party that acts as a facilitator and resolution seeker for the process.

Many people benefit from working with a Coach. Just like athletes use for sports! They prepare you mentally, physically, emotionally, financially, psychologically and even spiritually for the road ahead, peak performance during and recovery after.

This brings us to the topic of Coaches. There are **four types of coaches:**

A **Certified Divorce Coach** is trained to take you from:

- Decision to divorce – should I, or shouldn't I?
- Decisions about the process of divorce
- Questions to ask attorneys
- Getting financially organized
- Getting organized for responding to being served
- Parenting concerns during divorce
- How to answer children's questions
- Communicating with lawyer, spouse & others
- Getting ready for settlement discussions
- Getting ready for mediation
- Getting prepared for a court date
- Effectuating the settlement
- Taking on the new roles of ex-spouse and co-parent
- How to deal with moving
- Being stuck -letting go – moving on
- Developing your financial independence

- Developing a new or improved career
- Building a business
- Learning to date again
- Remarriage

Certified Divorce Specialist:

- Similar in scope as CDC but has the added skills and knowledge of Neuro Linguistic Programming approach to coaching Trauma-Informed clients.
- High Conflict Divorce Coach: Training specifically attuned to all aspects of divorcing high conflict couples, people, children, family dynamics, situations and events.

Other coaches to consider:

- **Certified Life Coach**- help with goals that pertain to all aspects of life change but do not have specific skills set in divorce
- **Career Transition Specialist**- planning, creation, execution of marketing, product, sales and customer satisfaction in all aspects of entrepreneurship and business development
- **Parenting Coordinator**...needs help with children with special needs, parents living in separate states or countries, estrangement and alienation cases. If you have a child with mild or severe learning or physical disabilities, it is your responsibility to document and secure their needs now.

Are you more secure on the other professionals in the process now? Now is the time to educate yourself and be confident that their needs are met.

NOTES

LESSON FOUR
FIND MENTAL HEALTH PROFESSIONALS

There are many times during the divorce process where stress, fear and overwhelm can take over...our minds race, our heart rate increases, our body tightens, our digestion suffers, our muscles ache ...and we begin to feel like we are falling apart.

It's time to see life as it truly is. It is time to accept that there is no shame in seeing a therapist or considering mental health care, including the need for medication.

Let's consider a few options.

Psychologist vs. Psychiatrist (if you need medication) specialists come in the name of therapist, counselor, clinician...and several other names I have not heard of yet. The field is growing and expanding day by day.

Therapy can help you process and accept the reality of divorce.

Medication can help you cope with extreme highs or lows, sleep and focus. I am not against pharmaceuticals for mental health. It may be needed ... but it could be advantageous to look at holistic options too!!
It's best to consider all of the options to walk you down the path towards healing and peace.

Here are a few **alternative therapies** to consider.

- Chiropractic
- Energy Work Practitioners

- Functional MDs
- Massage
- Reiki
- Yoga/Meditation teachers, and other modalities we have considered in past chapters.

Get out there and try a few options to see how they affect your physical and mental/emotional wellbeing.

DO something. Doing nothing is a sure sign that nothing will change, and things will only get worse.

Now…Let's dig into the professionals with whom you should be familiar to attain a custodial agreement and parenting plan.

In families where there is conflict, abuse or control, it may be necessary to call in the help of a **Licensed Clinical Social Worker** (LCSW). This is never anything we desire but something we know we need.

In situations where the wellbeing of the children is in danger or question, the court may appoint, or your spouse and lawyer may request the appointment of a **Guardian Ad Litem or "GAL"** to determine the competency of one or both of the parents. This is a stressful time. Be natural and relaxed if one comes to visit you. Spouses have been known to **insist** on one to add to the drama, intimidation, control and revenge of the other. GAL's are not evil; just know they are doing their job, be open-minded and allow options to unfold.

Child advocates and child advocate attorneys work to protect the rights of minors in cases involving divorce, child custody, neglect or abuse, and juvenile court proceedings. Courts will appoint a child advocate attorney in the following circumstances: Neglect/abuse of the minor and in contested child custody proceedings.

Family Reunification specialists can assist in Custody, Foster Parenting, Adoption, Immigration and Abuse cases. There is a need for sensitivity in the court system for children's needs to always be taken into consideration.

When making a custody decision, there are many facts to consider. If you and your spouse are not on the same page, it may be time to consult with children advocates to get their professional take on the situation, so the judge is not deciding for you.

 How does it feel to know more of the players in the process?
Who do you believe you need to help you and your children?

And next, we take a look at the financial experts in the process.

LESSON FIVE
FIND FINANCIAL EXPERTS

If you are in the dark about your finances, you need a financial expert. If you are in debt, you need a financial expert. If you have never handled taxes, budgets, expenses or investments, you need a financial expert.

Let's just face it …we all need to learn how to make, invest, save and responsibly pay our bills…and it's never too early in the process to understand the rules, laws and best practices. But the professional that REALLY understands how divorce will affect your finances is a **Certified Divorce Financial Analyst (CDFA). Divorce will affect every aspect of your finances. Every single one.**

I highly suggest having a Lifestyle Analysis to determine how your life before, during and after divorce will be affected and what you need to plan for. A consultation is usually free. It could save your future from disaster.

Bank professionals: get to know the people that work at the bank where you and your spouse have a checking, savings, loan, mortgage. They will be more likely to make copies, answer questions and give you facts if they know you. Yes, most documents can be found online now…but I can't tell you what a difference it makes when you have a personal relationship with the professionals that work in your bank.

1.   IF you can't seem to locate money
2.   IF bills are being paid with money that seems just to appear
3.   IF your spouse is buying expensive gifts, trips, clothes, jewelry and you don't know where the funds are coming from
4.   IF you aren't allowed to look at your tax returns
5.   IF you see things on your tax returns that are unfamiliar

It is time to visit a **Forensic Accountant**. They can hunt down the trail of funds and determine their origin. It is important now to know if they are marital or separate assets…such as a pension, real estate, investment, insurance policies, etc.

Let's work through a few common mistakes people make!

1. Do not trust!
2. Close all joint accounts with creditors
3. Or Freeze accounts that can't be closed to secure that funds are not used and dissipated.
4. It's now time to plan to grow your own SOLO individual accounts to protect YOUR credit.
5. It is widespread to see credit scores drop during divorce.
6. Do everything you can to protect your credit.
7. Does it matter if you have a CPA? CFP? Or CDFP? You need to know what to ask!
8. Grow and Protect credit by staying on top of your finances.

And what happens to the house? Where are we going to live? Trust the real estate professionals to help!

LESSON SIX
REAL ESTATE EXPERTS

Now that we have worked with the legal, mental health and financial professionals to consider…it's time to work with the professionals that will help you get creative with where you, you ex and your children will live.

Be sure to find a Real Estate Divorce Specialist CDRS or Real Estate Divorce Expert CDRE (more lengthy and credible course)

IF you own a home with your spouse, chances are it will need to be sold and equity divided. It is also possible to have one of the parties stay in the marital home if the finances can support it.

It is also possible to NEST, where the kids stay put and the parents alternate living in the house with the kids. (not for everyone) Keep in mind the "memories" may overpower the security.

It is not a bad idea to consider a downsize and a new beginning. If a sale is in the picture and children are also involved …this is a VERY sensitive time.

Of course, you want to try to get the highest sale you can to secure your future and new purchase…so it's time to clean, update, paint, declutter and downsize.

The beauty of a **Home Stager or Professional Home Organizer**?

This goes without saying. IF it's not in a budget…perhaps you have a friend who is a neat nick and fabulous decorator who can help lessen the load and overwhelm. A free consult may be worth the tips you will get—experience with the sensitivity of kids: toys, clothes, sports equipment.

Best to have Open Houses while kids are in school, sports or away with friends.

It's also best not to change too much of the kids' environment but to discuss a fresh new start instead of getting rid of things and throwing them out. Allow them to have input on any changes.

Why make sure your realtor has experience working with divorce sales and settlements? Not all RE experts are familiar with divorce proceedings, mortgages, tax ramifications and creative refinancing strategies.

What do you need help with? Most couples have a mortgage on their home when they divorce. If you do meet with a CDLP.

Mortgage and Title expert/Certified Divorce Lending Professional CDLP is an expert in how a divorce can effect your mortgage/s and ways to save money and keep or sell your home without penalties or financial loss. CDLP's are highly trained in all aspects of improving credit scores, mortgage eligibility, title transfers, quit claims, home equity and HECMP's for divorcing couples. I highly recommend working with one if you have a mortgage with your spouse you jointly own.

Other professionals to consider:

1. **Estate/Jewelry Appraiser**
2. **Property/Casualty Insurance Agent**
3. **Property Appraiser**
4. **Home Stager**
5. **Professional Home Organizer**

Each home situation is different, but aren't you glad you know there is help that can take away some of the confusion and pressure of knowing what your options are?

REVIEW

YOUR TEAM IS YOUR HERO

If you have come to the decision that you cannot mediate OR you need to do more homework to know for sure that mediation is a viable option, you need to create your holistic team to work with you.

1. Attorney (for legal advice and paperwork processed)
2. Mediator (for negotiated agreement)
3. Child advocate (parenting plan and child support)
4. CDFA (financial planning, taxes and alimony)
5. CDRE/CDLP Real Estate/Mortgage professionals (home analysis, appraisal and sales)
6. CDC to get you all through it with grace, less stress, speed and strength **to save time, money, relationships and heartache.**

It's essential to meet with who you think can help you and eliminate the ones that you don't need. Knowing your options is half the battle.

In Chapter Six, the focus is on the kids.

NOTES

6

LASTING IMPRESSIONS LAST A LIFETIME

DO RIGHT BY THE KIDS

I trusted the process. I trusted myself and my spouse to do the right thing. We had NO plan and it was a mess and our kids suffered as a result of our lack of preparation. I was in the dark about the damage to our children.

My parents stayed together for the children. They stayed together due to the religious doctrine we knew despite living parallel lives and treating each other with disregard.

I secretly wished my parents would divorce. When they stayed together, it truly felt worse (at the time). I imagined how life would be if they had been honest with each other and created better lives separately. I'll never know if that would have been reality…but the point here is that we all come to divorce with our own personal impressions and memories. Memories stick with you and they leave lasting impressions.

 **What are your impressions of divorce?**

1. Did your parents stay together?
2. Are they still married?
3. Did they stay together for the children?
4. Did they divorce?
5. Did they involve you in their pains and decisions?
6. How did you and your siblings handle the changes?
7. Did you take sides?
8. Did they alienate you from the other parent?
9. Did you have friends whose parents divorced?
10. How did they cope?
11. How did that make you feel?

You can see how your past experiences have left a mark on your soul and now YOU are facing these very same pains, questions and decisions that will affect the entire course of your future. Here we go digging into the importance of creating a **child-centered divorce** experience as best you can. It's time to think about the children.

Yes…we are going to get serious about how to center your divorce around your children. Because isn't that what really matters?

Telling the children mom and dad are divorcing is perhaps the hardest conversation you will ever have in your life. I still get a terrible feeling of guilt and terror when I think back to the day. I was not prepared for "the" conversation. This moment in time will forever stand out in your memory: some things we did wrong and some things we did right.

Let's break down the steps about how to tell, how to deal with custody conflicts, how to support them emotionally, how to protect them, how to answer their questions and the worst-case scenario of all…how to cope with Parent Alienation. This is a crucial module to absorb. Let's do this right…Let's do it for the kids.

LESSON ONE
CHILD-CENTERED DIVORCE

The focus now will shift from your needs and emotions to your children's needs and emotions.

You may ask yourself why we didn't delve into this earlier. Well, the answer is sometimes difficult to see, but if you are not doing well, there is no way your kids will be doing well. Children are sponges and they absorb everything they see, hear and feel in their home and environment.

They are more aware and attentive than we realize, and they have a strong intuitive sense of when something is going well, when something is going poorly …AND when something is just plain BAD.

The looks we give each other, the non-verbal body language we send, the way we ignore each other and treat each other with criticism, contempt, defensiveness, stonewalling, and projection.

If you are communicating well…and I do mean if…set out a time and place that both of you feel comfortable.

Make the decision together when to tell them, where to tell them, what to say to them, what NOT to say to them, if anyone else should be present…and anything else you want to create. The experience you create will leave one of the most important memories and impressions you make on them as parents and it's **one that you should do together.** This is one thing we did right. It was the rest of the process that we did wrong.

Now, I rely on my friend and expert Rosalind Sedacca, who created the term *A Child-Centered Divorce.*

Are you wondering:

1. When to break the news to your kids
2. Just how you're going to tell them?
3. Whether to do it alone or with your spouse?
4. And most important of all – are you unsure about … what you should say?

I've been there. And I stayed up for many sleepless nights trying to figure out the best way to break the news. Ultimately Rosalind came up with an innovative, yet simple new approach that was very successful for me and the hundreds of other families that have been using it since she launched her book. I am excited to share this approach with you. And I want to remind you that you're not alone. There are answers to your questions. There's also a simple way to tell your children in a manner that eases their pain, reassures them of your love and helps them get through the transition that lies ahead. Best of all …it's all in a book I highly recommend.

How Do I Tell the Kids about the Divorce? by **Rosalind Sedacca** is your answer.

Let's face it, telling your children about the divorce may be the most difficult conversation you'll ever have. Why leave it to chance? She wrote this guidebook, so you don't have to worry, spend sleepless nights or beat yourself up about making a mistake … saying the wrong things … falling apart … or not having answers to your children's immediate questions. I know there are many books about children and divorce. What makes this one unique? Her innovative Create-a-Storybook™ concept.

She prepares an actual template for you – the word-for-word text that tells you just what you need to say – in age-appropriate language for children 5 to 10 or 10 to 15. And then she guides you, step-by-step, in preparing an attractive personal family storybook, in a photo-album format, that your children will want to read. In other words, she doesn't just tell you what to say – she says it for you

– with love and compassion! She also includes the six key messages your children continuously need to hear, understand and accept at this crucial time.

Even if you don't purchase her guidebook, you need to **make sure you share these six essential messages with your kids again and again so that they never forget:**

1. **You are, and always will be, loved my Mom and Dad.**
2. **You are, and will continue to be, safe.**
3. **You are not to blame for any of this.**
4. **Mom and Dad will still always be your Mom and Dad.**
5. **This is about change, not about blame.**
6. **Everything is going to be okay.**

The **benefits for both you and your children** are immeasurable. After reading this Guidebook ...

You will feel:

1. Confident about how to begin, end, and know just what to say all the way through the "divorce" conversation
2. Prepared to share with your children the six essential concepts they need to understand and accept
3. Aware of what your children may be thinking and feeling so you can respond accordingly
4. Secure, as a role model for your children, on how to handle disagreements and discord with dignity, integrity and respect
5. Proud, for the sake of your children, that you took the high road as you venture into your separation or divorce
6. Empowered about conveying your message with understanding, compassion and love
7. Confident you're giving your family the best possible foundation for a healthy and harmonious future, despite your divorce
8. Capable of creating and maintaining a Child-Centered divorce

9. Ready to tell your kids about the divorce – because you will be!

You will know ...

1. How to avoid anxiety, awkwardness and stumbling for just the right words
2. You have a text you can refer back to so that you stay on track – even when emotions run high
3. How to communicate in the language your children (between the ages of 5 and 15) will understand – and appreciate
4. What to expect, how to respond and be prepared with answers to inevitable questions
5. That you are giving your children a wonderful storybook about them and their family. One that they will want to read over and over again for reassurance
6. How to access resources you can turn to, including articles, organizations, attorneys and therapists, to give you additional support in the coming months

You will be relieved that your kids will ...

1. Feel safe, loved and accepted during this challenging time in their lives
2. Know and understand they are not responsible or to blame for your divorce
3. Discover that change, while frightening and difficult, is inevitable and can turn out okay
4. Appreciate having a storybook about them and their family that they can read again and again for reassurance
5. Grasp, through text and family photographs, that life goes on from the past into the future, and there will be many happy experiences to look forward to ahead
6. Hear, and start to accept, the six key messages essential to help them through the divorce and beyond
7. Avoid the anxiety and guilt of having to make choices or decisions that are not their responsibility

Rosalind is the author of the *Parenting Beyond Divorce* guidebook, a 10-hour Mastering Child-Centered Divorce Audio Coaching Program with Workbook, an 8-hour Anger Management course for co-parents, several other eCourses and ebooks, dozens of articles and newsletters – as well as contributions to other people's books – on personal, family and business relationships.

She is my go-to parenting expert. I'm also wise enough not to be doing this alone! If you feel you need a template on how to tell the children, buy her book!!

Life will always be different.

It now means that there will be two households. It now means your children will be living with two sets of rules and expectations and freedoms.

This can cause conflict and confusion. I suggest you **control what you can and let go of what you cannot**.

I also suggest you use **a Co-Parenting APP** to communicate with instead of phone calls, text messages, emails and social media DM. All of which can get messy and ugly. There are eight or so good co-parenting apps and there is a new one coming out every month. Find the one that feels right for you and your family. (My Family Wizard and FAYR are my two favorites)

Please do not overlook the state-mandated **parent education program** in MOST states. If it is not mandated…find one, register for it…and go take it. It will prepare you for the road ahead in a practical way and you will realize you are not alone.

You may meet some other like-minded people who are also going through divorce. I encourage you to look forward to the parent education program instead of dreading it. There is a wonderful read available from Jessica Maldonado at MWI that talks through seven reasons to look forward to your parent education program. I'll summarize the key points here and you can read the full article at *https://www. mwi.org/look-forward-to-your-parent-education-program/*

Solo space for learning and reflection
Generally, spouses are not allowed to attend the parent programs together. This gives you the freedom to feel comfortable asking questions and sharing without it impacting on your divorce.
These programs also remind you of the importance of self-care. Something that is easily forgotten in the stress of divorce

A community of experienced parents and experts
Often others have traversed your path before you and can share the strategies that did and did not work for them. Even just the comfort of hearing where other parents in their journey can be a huge boon for you in your journey. The facilitators for your course are also qualified and experienced in mental health disciplines.

Helping you focus on your kids
There will always be an impact on children from divorce, but it doesn't have to be negative. The parenting programs will help you gain knowledge and skills to guide your children through the divorce process with love and empathy.

Supporting each child
Every child is different and reacts differently to divorce. Working through a parenting program can provide you with the best range of tools to have in your toolbox to deal with, no matter what your child throws at you.

Co-parenting tools and tips
Co-parenting is hard. It is difficult to parent together whilst living separately. These programs will help you navigate co-parenting, so you can work more easily with your co-parent/ex-partner.

Next: it's time to talk to the children's teachers, coaches, instructors and mentors. They should be informed that life is going to be different at home so that they can keep a special eye on your kids. They will pick on unusual behavior, sadness, anxiety, anger, exhaustion, drugs or alcohol usage...and any other oddities.

In the worst cases, one or both parents practice alienating comments, communication and gaslighting acts that are used to turn one parent against the other. It isn't hard to do.

If you are experiencing disrespect, anger, lies, ridicule, judgment... nip it in the bud and address it immediately. Make note of the conversation, what was said, when it was said, where it was said and in what context. Write the conversation or comments down so you recall the facts as best you can. Record the conversation if need be to prove that you are not making it up or lying.

If your children continue to act alienated, i.e., they no longer want to see you, they swear at you, say nasty things to you, call you names, avoid spending time with you, call you, ignore you or lie to you: **you need to seek professional help.**
If they demand money, or rides, or favors or things you don't approve of...with a threat or bullying attached to you. (i.e., I won't come to see you if you don't. You will never see your grandchildren if you don't. It's mine and you must give it to me, I am entitled to it...etc, etc., etc.)

Seek professional help with a **Parent Alienation expert** immediately. If you can prove that your children are being brainwashed, abused and being convinced not to see you...you have a case for custody.

Parent Alienation is child abuse. Children have a right to be loved by both parents and have the other parent encourage a strong bond with the other. Children become damaged when they no longer have a relationship with the other parent due to alienation. **Parental alienation is the process, and the result, of psychological manipulation of a child into showing unwarranted fear, disrespect or hostility towards a parent and/or other family members.**

It is not easy to fight or undo the damage and this can result in long term estrangement.

LESSON TWO
CUSTODY AND PARENTING PLANS

I was green when it came to custody.

Women are typically attached to their house and possessions. They see them as a part of their identity. Custody will play a significant role in who lives where.

Let's shift to understanding custody.

Joint physical custody and joint legal custody is best for the children if you can pull it off. It isn't easy if you are not in agreement on how to raise your children. In fact, it is one of the reasons marriages fall apart. If mom and dad do not see eye to eye on how to raise children, it can be complicated but that doesn't mean it is impossible.

 **Let's explore a few considerations.**

Topics like:

1. Babysitters? Nannies?
2. Bedtime: how late is too late? Co-sleeping?
3. Breastfeeding?
4. Cell phones?
5. Chores? Allowance?
6. Circumcision?

7. Diet/Meals: snacks? sugar/candy? rigid mealtimes? eat on the sofa watching TV? vegetarian, vegan?
8. Education: preschool, public versus private? boarding school?
9. Holidays: where to spend them? how to spend them? celebrate or not? how much to spend on gifts?
10. Homework: Do they have to do their homework to go outside and play? Video games?
11. How much to spend on children's clothes? Consignment? Donations?
12. Playdates? How often? How long? How many?
13. Religion: different religions, go to church, not go to church? religious education?
14. Sleepovers? Birthdays?
15. Sports and Activities: How many are too many? What sports are safe? How much is too much to spend?
16. Vaccinations? Anti-vac? Flu-shots?
17. What to name the children? Family names? Unusual names? Common names?
18. Vacations? Where to go? When to go? How much to spend? Who comes with us?
19. Pets? No pets? Cat? Dog? Both? Snake?
20. Video games? Social media? Internet usage?

The list goes on and on and on....

Children typically want to live with the parent who has fewer rules and is less fussy about the rules they do have. Kids like to feel like they can get away with whatever they can. Kids want to live with the "fun" parent.

Thank goodness the decision isn't up to the children.

Although at 14, the child has a say in the eyes of the court and can choose who they would prefer to live with.

If both parents cannot agree to create a set of guidelines and adhere to them and communicate respectfully with each other as the rules and guidelines need to be adjusted as the kids grow up and situations change ...it usually gets ugly.

It is possible, but not easy. This is one of the reasons it is best to use an APP for communication **and** scheduling and be sure to have a coach to keep you on task and not allow your emotions to get the best of you.

I encourage you to refrain from engaging in "text wars". It usually gets nasty real quick.

Now let's define a few terms you need to understand:

Child custody is a legal term regarding **guardianship,** which is used to describe the legal and practical relationship between a parent or guardian and a child in that person's care.

Child custody consists of legal custody, which is the right to make decisions about the child, and physical custody, which is the right and duty to house, provide and care for the child.

Married parents typically have joint legal and physical custody of their children. Decisions about child custody typically arise in proceedings involving divorce, annulment, separation, adoption or parental death.

In most jurisdictions, child custody is determined in accordance with the "**best interests of the child**" standard.

Following ratification of the United Nations Convention on the Rights of the Child in most countries, terms such as parental responsibility, "residence" and "contact" (also known as "**visitation**", "**conservatorship**" **or** "**parenting time**" in the United States) have superseded the concepts of "custody" and "access" in some member nations. Instead of a parent having "custody" of or "access" to a child, a child is now said to "reside" or have "contact" with a parent.

Legal custody involves the division of rights between the parents to make important life decisions relating to their minor children. Such decisions may include the choice of a child's school, physician, medical treatments, orthodontic treatment, counseling, psychotherapy and religion. Legal custody may be joint, in which case both parents share decision-making rights, or sole, in which case one parent has the rights to make critical decisions without regard to the wishes of the other parent

Physical custody establishes where a child lives and who decides day-to-day issues regarding the child

If a parent has physical custody of a child, that parent's home will typically be the child's legal residence (domicile).

The times during which parents provide lodging and care for the child are defined by a court-ordered custody parenting schedule, also known as a parenting plan.

The different forms of physical custody include:

1. **Sole custody**, an arrangement whereby only one parent has physical custody of the child. The other non-custodial parent would typically have regular visitation rights.
2. **Joint physical custody**, a shared parenting arrangement where both parents have the child for approximately equal amounts of time, and where both are custodial parents.
3. **Bird's nest custody**, a type of joint physical custody whereby the parents go back and forth from a residence in which the child always resides, placing the burden of upheaval and movement on the parents rather than the child.

4. **Split custody,** an arrangement whereby one parent has sole custody over some children, and the other parent has sole custody over the remaining children.

5. **Alternating custody**, an arrangement whereby the child lives for an extended period with one parent and an alternate amount of time with the other parent. This type of agreement is also referred to as Divided custody.

6. **Third-party custody**, an arrangement whereby the children do not remain with either biological parent or are placed under the custody of a third person.

7. **Joint physical custody, aka Shared parenting:** Joint physical custody, or shared parenting, means that the child lives with both parents for equal and/or approximately equal amounts of time. In joint custody, both parents are custodial parents and neither parent is non-custodial. With joint physical custody, terms such as "primary custodial parent" and "primary residence" have no legal meaning other than for determining tax status. The term "visitation" is not used in joint physical custody cases, but only for sole custody orders. In joint physical custody, the actual lodging and care of the child is shared according to a court-ordered custody schedule, also known as a parenting plan or parenting schedule.

8. **Sole physical custody** means that a child resides with only one parent while the other parent may have visitation rights with his/her child. The former parent is the custodial parent, while the latter is the non-custodial parent.

Only 60% of children live with both parents in the USA.
That means 40% do not!

Let's compare.

Comparing 36 western countries in 2005/06, Thoroddur Bjarnason studied the proportion of 11-15-year-old children living in different child custody arrangements.

The percent of children living in intact families with both their mother and father were highest in Macedonia (93%), Turkey (89%), Croatia (89%) and Italy (89%), while it was lowest in the United States (60%), Romania (60%), Estonia (66%) and Latvia (67%).

In the other anglophone countries, it was 70% in the United Kingdom, 71% in Canada and 82% in Ireland.

Among the children who did not live with both their parents, the percent in a shared parenting versus sole custody arrangement was highest in Sweden (17%), Iceland (11%), Belgium (11%), Denmark (10%), Italy (9%) and Norway (9%). At 2% or less, it was lowest in Ukraine, Poland, Croatia, Turkey, the Netherlands and Romania.

It was 5% in Ireland and the United States and 7% in Canada and the United Kingdom.

Shared parenting is increasing in popularity. By 2016/17, the percentage in Sweden had risen to 34% of the 6-12-year-old age group and 23% among 13-18-year-old children.

Jurisdiction
A child custody case must be filed in a court that has jurisdiction over the child custody disputes.

Jurisdiction normally arises from the presence of the children as legal residents of the nation or state where a custody case is filed.

However, some nations may recognize jurisdiction based upon a child's citizenship even though the child resides in another country or may allow a court to take jurisdiction over a child custody case either on a temporary or permanent basis based upon other factors.

"Forum shopping" may occur both between nations and where laws and practices differ between areas within a nation.

If a plaintiff files a legal jurisdiction that the plaintiff believes to have more favorable laws than other possible jurisdictions, that plaintiff may be accused of forum shopping.

The Hague Convention seeks to avoid this, also in the United States of America, the Uniform Child Custody Jurisdiction and Enforcement Act was adopted by all 50 states, family law courts were forced to defer jurisdiction to the home state.

The "best interest" rule. In the context of cases regarding custody, the "best interest" rule suggests that all legal decisions made to accommodate the child are made to ensure a child's happiness, security and overall well-being.

Many different factors go into the decision that made in a child's best interests, which include:

1. **the child's health**
2. **environment**
3. **social interests**
4. **the relationship each parent has with the child**
5. **the ability of each parent to address the needs of the child.**

One problem with the "best interest" rule is that it has been a standard in determining child custody for the most recent 40 years in history. Although it has been so widely favored amongst legal systems, there are some deficiencies to the concept.

Robert Mnookin, an American lawyer, author, and Professor of Law at Harvard Law School claimed that the **best interest rule is indeterminate. It is a broad and vague set of guidelines that only lead to increased conflict amongst the parents instead of promoting cooperation that would lead to meeting the best interests of the child.**

Some of these problems specifically include:

1. The current test for best interest generates high costs, which can impose on both the court and opposing parties.
2. The verifiability of the best interest standard is hard to achieve.
3. The privacy of family life makes assessing the evidence provided difficult.

The best interest's standard only worsens the problem, in which both parties are encouraged to introduce evidence of the quality of their parenting (which also promotes trying to disprove the opposing party's capabilities of taking the child into custody).

In an example of divorce, both parties are experiencing high levels of stress, which could make for a poor basis for assessing family behaviors and relationships. To better analyze the "best interest" of children, several experiments were conducted to observe the opinions of children themselves.

Children of divorce were found to want equal time with both of their parents.

Studies conducted by Wallerstein, Lewis and Blakeslee (2002) show that children from all age ranges indicate that equal or shared parenting is of their **best interest 93 percent of the time.**

Several other studies were able to produce similar results, including Smart (2002), Fabricus and Hall (2003), Parkinson, and Cashmore and Single (2003).

As a result, there has been a **push to allow for joint custody of children** in the most recent years, which strives to meet the interests of the children best and most evidently favors a gender-neutral stance on the custody issue.

However, **the decision is highly situational,** for joint custody can only be achieved in the absence of certain exceptions. For example, a history of domestic violence found from either parent can most certainly trump the possibility of joint custody for a child.

As you can clearly see, according to the experts, custody is a highly emotional and challenging decision. Some parents will go to any length to have full, **sole custody just to spite the other parent.**

Some parents allow the kids to stay where they are comfortable to allow them the greatest amount of stability and familiarity.

Some parents will do anything they can to prevent the other parent from being involved in decision making and see them as the enemy.

Custody can be modified. It does require filing a motion to modify with the court. Evidence/proof is required to ask for a modification. (Change of job, change in work schedule, moving out of state, financial hardship, illness, re-marriage (stepchildren), to name a few. If small changes can be made without involving the courts ...do so. It will cost you money and upset in court to do so. This is where the **APPs can be helpful.**

Parenting plans make life BETTER and allow parents options!

If you can split your time 50/50, this is ideal. It doesn't work for everyone, but let's look at how that would work out.

Deciding if a 50/50 schedule will work for you:

1. There are many factors to consider when deciding what schedule will best fulfill the physical, social, and emotional needs of your child.

2. 50/50 schedules can benefit a child because the child spends substantial time living with both parents. This allows him or her to build a close relationship with both parents, and to feel cared for by both parents.

3. 50/50 schedules work best when:

    •   The parents live relatively close to each other, so exchanges are more straightforward.

    •   The parents can communicate with each other about the child without fighting.

    •   The child can handle switching between parents' homes.

    •   Both parents are committed to putting the child's best interests first.

    •   The parents agree that the 50/50 schedule is the best one for their children.

Along with your residential schedule, you may want to include a **holiday schedule** or a **summer break schedule** in your parenting time arrangements. These schedules may change the percentage of time each parent has with the children. If you have a residential schedule that isn't 50/50, you can use a holiday or seasonal schedule to make parenting time closer to equal. You can also include 3rd party time in your schedule that shows when your child isn't with either parent.

Marking when the child is in school or daycare can more accurately show when each parent has quality parenting time, and it can change the parenting timeshare percentages. Communication makes co-parenting work or not!!

I use **Divorceify**'s templates. Sonia Queralt and her team have created the best templates. They are interactive and save hours of confusion. There are numerous creative schedules you can play with to see what works for you.

 You can download the Divorceify templates from the resources page at: https://betterdivorceacademy.com/resources/. See if any of the suggested plans would suit your family.

I also like the APP's: CustodyXchange, Twohouses, TalkingParents, Weparent, Alimentor, AppClose, TimeTree, Fayr, OurFamilyWizard....and a new one will come out each month!!

I wish we had one of these. You have no idea.

It would have saved us years of anguish, yelling, text wars, alienation and pain.

LESSON THREE
HOW TO SUPPORT THE KIDS

By now, you are getting an idea about how to protect the kids best. Including, how to tell them and what the terms of custody mean.

It's time to shift our thinking to the ins and outs of child support. The history of child support goes back to the days of English law being imposed in the US as far back as 1604. The laws were refined and became more detailed throughout the 1950s, 60's 70's, but it wasn't until the 1998 "Deadbeat" Parents Law…the law gave punishment for non-payment for up to two years imprisonment and $10,000 fine.

The welfare of children is the cornerstone of child support.

Children need not know what child support is, who pays and who receives, how much the parent is receiving, when it is paid and if it is not paid.

Giving them this information is **truly damaging to them** and it pits one parent against the other. Resist the temptation to tell the children any details about child support. **All they need to know is that they will be cared for to the best of both parents' abilities and that both parents love them and care for them.**

At the beginning of the divorce proceedings or mediation meeting, custody needs to be determined.

Temporary child support is determined in all 50 states by each state's child support calculator.

Judges also have discretion when it comes to special circumstances that would warrant deviating from the states' formula. (i.e., medical expenses) **Child support is calculated by a form you can get online in each state**. There isn't much left to the imagination anymore. There truly is a formula. Employment and income, assets and debts, the cost of health insurance coverage and other medical expenses and childcare expenses are all taken into consideration.

Custody typically will determine what each parent will pay and contribute towards child support. If both parents work and their income is close to the same, they will both contribute equally. Health insurance will be deducted from the parent who pays for it. Additional expenses like schooling, childcare, sports, extracurricular activities are also taken into consideration. Extracurricular activities are usually considered at 7% of child support (but is unique in each state)

Temporary child support can be beneficial, while the details of the divorce are worked out. This establishes a pattern of ability to pay, and what is in the best interest of the children.

Temporary orders can transition into permanent orders...so take great care and consideration into where the children will reside and who is paying what. Child support is typically paid weekly. For example, every Friday by Noon by direct deposit to the custodial parent. This date can be agreed upon by both parties. If not, the judge will decide for you.

I highly suggest you download and use the APP My Family Wizard or FAYR that I suggested earlier.

It is NEVER fun to go to court to tell the judge or a case manager that your spouse is ignoring or refusing to pay child support. If this happens, don't take it personally. It's good to let a day or so go by... or a week if you have communicated that there is a delay and why. It is advised not to let too much time go by, or they will usually take advantage of your patience and good nature and will do it again and again and again.

It is not unusual for payments to be overlooked, late or insufficient funds. You will need to keep track of these payments for proof that they were paid OR were not paid. If you need to file a contempt charge for court-ordered non-payment, you will need evidence of dates and amounts that were not paid.

If a spouse is injured and accumulates medical expenses, loses a job, or faces some other type of hardship…an adjustment or modification is considered by the courts.

It is usually a bad day in court when you must take your spouse to court and ask them to adjust your support. The court does not view this highly and can usually give some relief for a short period of time, but it is in the best interest of the children that child support is not suspended.

Phew…this is not an easy hearted topic, but it's so crucial that you truly understand how child support is viewed, calculated, paid and modified.

In most states, child support ends at the age of 18 and when they graduate from high school, but in other states, child support ends at the age of 23 or after they graduate from higher education.

 Now is the time to understand the laws in your state and **do your research,** so you know what you will likely be paying or receiving.

Excellent job! Be sure to download the child support calculator in your state and do the math. No one likes to be surprised!!

NOTES

LESSON FOUR
ALIMONY (AKA SPOUSAL SUPPORT)

We are ready to look at the topic of Alimony or what is more commonly known as Spousal Support.

The laws have changed recently, so it's essential to have a good understanding of them. Plus how the new laws have affected the way alimony is awarded and how the courts view it.

As of December 31, 2018…the law changed. Alimony awarded after this date is no longer deductible for the payer, AND alimony awarded after this date is no longer taxable for the payee. Alimony awarded before this date is not affected **by** this new law as long as it still meets the criteria. (9 steps)

This makes alimony more challenging to agree to due to the loss of the tax deduction and more appealing since it is no longer taxable income.

This will make a **one payment settlement much more appealing** for most payers.

For payments required under divorce or separation instruments that are executed after Dec. 31, 2018, the new law eliminates the deduction for alimony payments. Recipients of affected alimony payments will no longer have to include them in taxable income.

This "Tax Cuts and Job Act" treatment of alimony payments will apply to payments that are required under divorce or separation instruments that are:

1. Executed after Dec. 31, 2018, or
2. Modified after that date, if the modification specifically states that the TCJA treatment of alimony payments (not deductible by the payer and not taxable income for the recipient) now applies.

For individuals who must pay alimony, this change can be expensive--because the tax savings from being able to deduct alimony payments can be substantial. This is a game-changer for so many divorcing couples. So, you ask…how is alimony awarded?

 **The questions considered before awarding support:**

1. How many years have the couple been married?
2. Contribution to the marriage?
3. Income formula? Who makes who much?
4. The health of parties?
5. Earning ability and skills of each party?
6. Where are Children living?
7. Spousal waste or mismanagement of funds?
8. Who will be paying?

There is NO formula for alimony like there is for child support.

Some judges consider 1/3 of the higher income earner's salary to as a formula, but there is no law requiring that guideline.

1. Alimony generally is not awarded for couples married for fewer than ten years.
2. Alimony is usually awarded for couples married 20 or more years.
3. Traditionally alimony was 1/3 of the higher income spouse. Those days are gone.

BUT again, this is at the **total discretion of the judge.** Each judge brings to the table their own bias and history in awarding it and there is no guarantee that any amount will be awarded.

Now, if you are the one paying alimony (it's isn't a man's world anymore as women who are the breadwinners are paying too), it will mean a lifestyle change for you.

If you are the recipient, do not see alimony as a lottery win. The money is being awarded to you for your security, your education and to get you back on your feet.

Find an excellent experienced financial planner and plan, plan, plan for the day when it ends, is modified or adjusted. It is not time to blow it on a spending spree and go on nonstop vacations. It's time to create a plan for investing, saving and reevaluating your skills for the day when you are ready to take on a new career, start a business or retire. **Preparation for the future begins NOW.**

During most divorces that are dragged out and litigated, the average amount of time for the proceedings to occur ranges between 8-14 months. This is the time "temporary orders" are mandated by a judge in your case.

Whatever the amount, see this as an indication that your permanent order will be in a similar light. (usually within 10-15% higher or lower) IF you are making out well on the temporary amount, chances are good that the permanent amount will be in the same light.

You must prove that your needs are greater to receive more, of course, your spouse will ALWAYS try to prove that you are living in the lap of luxury and that you don't require 90% of what was awarded you.

Live within your budget, keep every receipt and prove that you are using the money to secure your future. Education, home, and business are positive improvements.

If you do receive Alimony, do not take it for granted. It can disappear in the blink of an eye and it's never forever.

- Use it wisely.
- Use it for your education.
- Use it to build your resume.
- Use it for a home.
- Use it for security.
- Use if for a business opportunity.

Nothing else.

And KEEP TRACK of it.
- When it is paid.
- How it is paid.
- And yes…if there are some bumps in the road with missed payments.

You will need that for court if you need to file a contempt motion.

You will have to weigh the pros and cons of filing a contempt of court motion for non-compliance.
If one week goes by, you may think it was an oversight…or an error in the bank's hands.
If two weeks go by, you might think it's a game your ex is playing.

But if more and more time passes and you let it go…they now have a reason to believe you can live without it and they can ask for it to be modified. (lessened)

If you freak out the minute it is late or overlooked or worse yet, deliberately missed, there could be some backlash.

Your ex may play sweet and innocent.

- I am not sure what you are talking about.
- Ignore you completely.
- It's the bank's fault.

- I don't have the money.
- I am working as hard as I can.
- What do you think I am made of money?
- Get a job...etc. etc. etc.

Or try to drag the kids into it.

- Your mother is taking all my money.
- I don't have any money to buy --
- Ask your mother. She took all my money.
- She took all my money to support her mother or boyfriend
- Your mother is lazy and doesn't want to work so I can work like a dog and pay all her bills, so she can....

You get the idea.

You will have to balance the mood of your ex and your need to pay your bills. If you are using the money wisely, there will be no backlash or less backlash. If you are going on vacations, expensive dinners and shopping spree, expect the worst.

There is one word of wisdom with alimony. Try to get the judge to order **DIRECT AUTOMATIC DEPOSIT.**

If payments are not made, you will have to file a contempt charge. It is not uncommon for a check to appear a day or two before the court date in front of the judge. It will cost in legal fees...but it is the only way for compliance with a court order. Pay or jail. You can see how easy and quick it can get nasty.

If you can negotiate or meditate a lump sum alimony payout...do it! It is always the best...unless you are headed for a litigated trial. It is also essential to protect yourself with a life insurance policy in case your ex passes away and you are left broke because alimony ends at death, remarriage or cohabitation of more than 90 days.

Alimony is a "dirty" word in the world of divorce. Sadly, spousal support is seen as some sort of charity.

You will get through it to get yourself back on your feet. Keep your chin high and create the life you desire and deserve. It is no one's business but yours. Live with integrity and self-love. The rest will fall into place.

Remember, divorce is a marathon, not a race. You are preparing yourself for the next best chapter of your life. It's time to buckle up and prepare for the waiting game. You got this and I have your back.

LESSON FIVE
THE WAITING GAME

You may want to hurry up and get it over with, but expect that it's a slow legal act that will take a while.

At the exact time in your life when you want to push through and get on with it and get it over with …the nature of the beast is forcing you to stop and slow down. The nature of the legal formality forces us to stop dead in our tracks and redefine our definition of patience.

As much as you want to push forward, rush through the process and be done with it…the paperwork, discovery and settlement process is a tedious and trying time. If you are a patient person, I dare you to not see yourself as challenged and to those of you who are impatient, there are NO WORDS. You will be tested at every decision, every meeting and every corner of the journey.

IF you are impatient… expect this process to be the death of you. It is now that you need to practice non-attachment and **use every possible tool you can utilize** to let go of your nature to control the outcome. **The legal system is not at all concerned nor interested in your emotions.**

Now is the time to let go of any attempt to control the paperwork process and the players. Regardless of the type of divorce process, you and your spouse decide to proceed with the amount of paperwork and procedure that is involved is ridiculous. Yes…much of which is to protect both parties, BUT it truly is in no way pleasant nor easy.

So how do you deal with such a stressful time without losing your mind, screaming and saying things you will no doubt regret?

YOU NEED to find the right experts to support your ability to make smart, mindful decisions and amp up your ability to handle stress and improve your wellness at all costs.

You will be keeping a watchful eye on your spouse throughout the divorce process and you better believe your spouse will be keeping a watchful eye on you. (and this is just another reminder to stay off social media)

There is nothing they will overlook or ignore to be to their benefit...

- You are spending too much
- You are hanging out with irresponsible people
- You are staying out too late
- You are leaving the kids home alone or with a babysitter too long
- You are not where they think you should be
- You are drinking too much
- You are posting happy times on social media when they think you should be home crying

There is NOTHING you will do that is not under scrutiny.

It's time to implore exceptional patience and compassion.

- First for yourself.
- Second for your spouse.

No, you do not need to lock yourself in a closet and DO NOTHING until the divorce is over, but you do need to heed all your actions and reactions with caution and compassion.

This is your time to stay close to home.

This is your time to step into your power and practice wellness and self-care. This is your time to read, study and determine your best self and future actions.

 **Can you practice the love you have for your kids and yourself MORE than the hate you have for your spouse???**

Can you let go of the past and step into the light of the future life you deserve and desire?

Can you live in alignment with your best self and heal the old parts of you that wanted healing and validation from your spouse?

Working with a Certified Divorce Coach will help you get out of your story and move you to a place of contentment, forward-thinking and creating your best life. The waiting game is time to keep moving forward.

Each day commit to taking one tiny baby step forward and never look back in a state of regret.

I cannot reinforce enough the **commitment you need to create the better future you deserve.**

My divorce took eight years. If you told me at the beginning of the journey that I would just be coming out at the end 8 years later…I would have thrown in the towel. I had in my mind's eye a one- to two-year process and a peaceful and fair outcome for myself, my spouse and our children. Divorce is, in so many ways a comparison to enduring childbirth. We enter the birthing unit in an individual state of preparedness…and with the roll of the dice, we have no idea what we are going to get.

A 20-minute labor and birth in the cab on the way to the hospital, a 2-hour stint just barely making it through the admittance process, a 12 hour birth with the whole family present, a 24 hour stalled labor then ends up in an "emergency" C-section or a marathon of walking up and down hallways and birthing on your terms.

Divorce can take so many different forms.

The difference here is that we, as women do not appear to be in charge of the process.

We are at the mercy of the legal system, lawyers or our spouse who takes over and tells us what we are going to settle for. The waiting game is where they say the rubber meets the road, or we separate the men from the boys…OR any other saying that tells us the road ahead is going to force you to access a strength you didn't even know you had. You are not as vulnerable as they want you to believe you are.

You got this. Keep your cool, practice extreme self-care and know you are worthy of the outcome you desire.

Last…we will tackle, in my opinion the most difficult result of divorce…alienation.

Take a deep breath …we will get through it together.

NOTES

LESSON SIX
PARENT ALIENATION AND ESTRANGEMENT

I had no idea what parent alienation was. I knew divorce with children ages 5-15 wasn't easy, but I had NO idea. So many of my clients believe that their spouse could never and would never do or say anything to turn their children against them, but it is more common than sitting at a red light.

Do not retaliate by saying bad things back about them.

Rise above it.

Let's see where this is coming from.

1. Our partners are angry.
2. Our partners are sad.
3. Our partners are revengeful.
4. Our partners are cheap.
5. Our partners are selfish.
6. Our partners are narcissists.
7. Our partners are mean.
8. Our partners are lost.
9. Our partners are desperate.
10. Our partners have lost sight of the love that once created the children we will always share and do not care what they have to do to hurt us and get back at us…even if that means hurting our own children.

And saying mean, hurtful and judgmental things about the other parent are the only ways they feel they have when they are disparate to get back at the other parent when they feel they are losing ground.

And you ask me: "How do I fight it?"

1. First, DO NOT take it personally.
2. Even though it is personal.
3. Even if it feels personal.
4. Even though it breaks you down to the very core of who and what you are… do not take it personally.

It is their stuff that they need to deal with. YOU DO NOT need to deal with their stuff. Let it go, let it go, let it go. Take a long, slow, deep, full, even, circular breath and let it GO.

According to Wikipedia …

> *Parental alienation describes a process through which a child becomes estranged from a parent as the result of the psychological manipulation of another parent.*

That sounds so evil and mean…and it is.

But how can that happen?

Well…when one parent continuously insults, judges, forms an alliance against, compares, degrades, ignores, criticizes, blames and disregards the other parent …it's easy. The child's estrangement may manifest itself as fear, disrespect or hostility toward the parent, and may extend to additional relatives or parties. Most children pull away from a parent at the onset of one parent moving out…but children are naturally curious and want to know about, hear about, see and spend time with BOTH parents.

If ONE parent is disregarding the other, the child will naturally show curiosity and an interest in the other. If the parent is agreeable and supportive of the other parent, the child will feel happy and satisfied with the situation.

> *Definition of Parental Alienation: The manipulation of a child to reject one parent or the other.*

If the parent is adversarial about the other parent, the child will feel sad, confused, and disappointed. IF this criticism continues, the child is likely to feel denial. The child's estrangement is disproportionate to any acts or conduct attributable to the alienated parent.

Parental alienation can occur in any family unit but is believed to occur most often within the context of family separation, particularly when legal proceedings are involved. However, the participation of professionals such as lawyers, judges and psychologists may also contribute to conflict.

In the eyes of the law, children need to have a good relationship with both parents and to achieve that, each parent should have significant quality time with the child.

Unfortunately, divorce is usually an ugly affair, and many parents allow their **anger to spill over** into the lives of their children. When a parent takes steps to isolate a child, make the child angry with, or afraid of, the other parent, it is called alienation.

The **primary weapons** parents use to alienate their children against the other parent include:

1. *Badmouthing* – Actively or casually allowing the children to overhear the parent speak about the divorce: This includes criticizing and belittling the other parent or telling the child that the other parent is dangerous, crazy, or somehow unworthy of the child's love.
2. *Interfering with the Child's Contact* – This includes delivering the child to the other parent late or picking him up early. Making excuses to keep the child during the other parent's scheduled time, refusing to allow the child to call or otherwise contact the other parent, or excessively calling the child while he is with the other parent.
3. *Causing the Child to Reject the other Parent* – This includes making the child feel guilty for loving the other parent, creating conflict between the child and the other parent,

forcing the child to choose between his parents, talking to the child about inappropriate matters (details of the marriage or divorce).

4. ***Undermining the Child's Relationship with the other Parent.*** This includes drilling the child for details of his visit with the other parent or asking the child to spy on the other parent, encouraging the child to call that parent by his or her first name, changing the child's name to exclude the other parent.

5. ***Undermining the other Parent's Role in the Child's Life*** – This includes refusing to provide the other parent information regarding the child's schooling, medical care, and activities. Refusing to notify the school, sports team coaches, doctors, and others of the other parent's contact information. Having a step-parent refer to him/herself as "Mom" or "Dad" when dealing with the school, teachers, coaches, doctors, and others. Plus refusing to invite the other parent to important activities such as birthday parties, graduation, parent-teacher conferences, school plays or concerts, and the like.

6. **Sharing documentation** and facts about the divorce to influence the children's views and opinions of the other parent.

7. **Asking the children** what the parent should do, giving the child a sense of power and authority.

Signs of Parental Alienation.

Every child has a need for, and right to, a close and loving relationship with both parents.

Children who have been forcibly separated from a parent – assuming there has been no abuse by that parent – have been found to be **highly sensitive to post-traumatic stress.**

Children who are the victims of parental alienation exhibit certain signs of parental alienation, and the true emotional and psychological damage that have been inflicted on them.

Anger – Expressed toward the target parent. Being exposed to the **criticisms and accusations** of one parent against the other causes a great deal of stress in children for which they have no outlet.

They develop **poor skills for dealing with conflict** and emotional pain and become quick to anger.

Lack of Self Esteem or Self Confidence – Being made to believe one parent is somehow bad or unworthy leads the child to believe that half of himself is also unworthy. This shows a serious lack of self-esteem, which can lead to destructive behaviors.

Lack of Impulse Control – Alienated children may lack the personal control necessary to evaluate situations before choosing an action. This can cause them to lash out in anger, or to engage in spur-of-the-moment impulsive behaviors, such as fighting, throwing things, or making rash choices.

Separation Anxiety – Children who are "programmed" by one parent to hate, fear, or distrust the other often show anxiety about leaving or being separated from the programming parent. This anxiety not only manifests when spending time with the other parent, but when the child attempts to participate in other activities, such as slumber parties, or summer camp.

Fears and Phobias – Some alienated children develop fears of things that may take them away from the "good" parent (the programmer), such as going to school. They sometimes begin making up physical illnesses as a way to remain at home – and to keep the parent at home with them.

Depression and Suicidal Thoughts – Parental alienation increases the pain of divorce for the children, leading to depression and even suicide.

Sleep Disorders – Children may find it difficult to sleep, or even have bad dreams, as they both worry about the dangers the target parent poses and feel guilt over their roles in the alienation.

Eating Disorders – In their attempts to gain control over their life and their parents' behaviors, many alienated children develop eating disorders, such as anorexia, bulimia, and obesity.

Problems in School – Alienated children tend to have more problems in school, from an inability to concentrate, to difficulties remembering what is taught. They may also get in trouble often for misbehaving.

Drug and Alcohol Abuse – Even at very young ages, alienated children have a greater danger of using drugs and alcohol, which often leads to other illegal activities.

Parental Alienation Syndrome. When a parent continually engages in strategies or acts to alienate a child from the other parent, serious damage to the child's psyche is likely. Pressured by the alienating parent, many children succumb and choose a side. This leads to certain irregular behaviors of a psychological issue known as "Parental Alienation Syndrome."

These include:

Campaign of Denigration – Upon choosing a side, the child becomes obsessed with the targeted parent's faults, and with hating that parent. This initial step occurs so quickly that the targeted parent is often stunned by the about-face taken by his or her child.

Hating a parent that has abused the child is considered to be justified and logical and is therefore not a sign of Parental Alienation Syndrome ("PAS").

Absurd, Weak, or Frivolous Reasons for Denigration – The complaints made by the child during his campaign of denigration are often irrational, or not sufficiently serious to normally cause a child to hate a parent. For instance, a child might state, as his primary reason for hating the targeted parent, that the parent does not allow him to eat spicy foods, or to see certain types of movies.

Lack of Ambivalence – Normal development of children involves some level of ambivalence – or uncertainty – about both parents. No parent is perfect, and children are prone to frustration and resentment for the limits they set.

A child suffering from Parental Alienation Syndrome does not express ambivalence about the alienating parent. Instead, the child automatically and reflexively throws himself into supporting that parent, showing no mixed feelings about pushing away, or hating, the targeted parent.

A child suffering from PAS sees one parent as all good and the other as all bad.

Independent Thinker and Decision-Maker – **When questioned about his extreme views of the targeted parent, and about the alienating parent's actions, a child suffering from PAS often insists that his feelings are entirely his own.** For instance, the child might call his father, whom the mother has been engaged in a campaign of alienation, to say, "I don't want to come to your house anymore. Mom had nothing to do with this decision. I made it all on my own." **The alienating parent is quick to protect the child's "right" to choose if he wants to visit his parent.**

No Guilt – Children suffering from PAS commonly claim that the targeted parent does not "deserve" to see them. The child does not feel bad about shutting the parent out and expresses no gratitude for the things that the parent does for him, or the gifts given.

Many children suffering from PAS will attempt to manipulate the situation, getting whatever they can from the targeted parent, with the absolute belief they are entitled to such gifts because the targeted parent is such a terrible person.

PAS children can be selfish, manipulative, and cruel.

Absolute Support of Alienating Parent – PAS children are unwilling to have an impartial view of disputes between parents. Such a child reflexively supports the alienating parent, refusing to even listen to the targeted parent's point of view.

Borrowed Scenarios – In their communications with the targeted parent, or with court officials, PAS children often spout phrases and ideas that come directly from the alienating parent's dialogue. The younger the child, the more likely his conversation contains words and ideas that he cannot even understand.
As an example of parental alienation syndrome, a child might claim that he hates his father because he is a "womanizer," having no idea what a womanizer is.

Hostility Toward Targeted Parent's Extended Family – At some point, it is typical for a child suffering from PAS to extend his hatred of the targeted parent to that parent's extended family. The child will similarly make complaints about these family members, which may include grandparents, aunts, and uncles, and even refuse to see them. PAS children often grow up missing important family events, such as weddings, funerals, birthdays, and anniversaries.

How to Prove Parental Alienation – Because alienation of a child against a parent has lasting harmful effects, it is taken very seriously by the family court system. In fact, a parent who actively alienates his or her children against the other parent is very likely to lose custody of those children and may even be restricted to supervised visitation. A parent who is being targeted for alienation has the right and responsibility of informing the court, though he or she will need to prove parental alienation.

Taking specific steps will help a parent prove parental alienation.

These include:

Keep a Journal – Write down any issues that occur when communicating with the alienating parent, and things said by the children that have obviously come from the other parent's mouth. Record dates and times of irregularities in visitation, such as plans being made by the other parent that conflict with visitation, failure to deliver the children as scheduled, and other happenings.

Record the Children's Actions – It is important to write down aberrant behavior and comments made by the children, which demonstrate the issue of alienation.

Record Special Requests or Changes Requested by the Alienating Parent – Alienating parents often ask changes to be made to visitation schedules, as well as to occasions with the children, then blame the targeted parent.

Pay Attention to Warning Signs – Be aware of the signs that a child is suffering from Parental Alienation Syndrome. Keep a record of suspect behaviors, including dates, times, and specific words or actions. Be aware of whether the child has "secrets" with the alienating parent. It is not uncommon for such parents to tell the child to keep something perfectly innocent, such as attending a baseball game, secret to build a bond with the child.

Maintain Open Communications with the Child. It is vital for both parents to maintain open communication with their children, making it clear that both parents love them. This does not mean to grill or interrogate the children about the other parent, but to engage in conversation on a variety of topics. The child may say something like, "Mom said you were too busy for me to come over last weekend," or express some other ideas being pumped into him by the other parent.

Enforce all Custody Orders – While this includes actual visitation dates and times, it also includes sharing information about the children. For instance, custody orders commonly require both parents to allow the other access to the child's education records and school activities, as well as medical records and medical appointments. Denying a parent access to such things is seen as being contrary to the child's best interests.

Once all the evidence has been gathered, the targeted parent can file a motion with the court to review or change child custody orders. In some cases, the court may appoint a GAL (guardian ad litem) to represent the child's best interests, separate from the representation of the parents.

Do not overlook the need to document and record what's been said. And do find advocates to defend accusations that are said against you.

What is the best way to cope? Start by backing off from all aggressive behavior. Do not engage in arguments of any kind. Simply agree to disagree and try your very best to disengage from any conflict.

As challenging as it is and how emotionally charged our ex may be (passive-aggressive or covert) step back and observe the confrontation and let it go. Stick to a schedule and let their anger and nastiness go at all costs.

If necessary, USE an APP for all communication and go **NO or LOW contact. Being a parent does not require you to subject yourself to abuse from your spouse or EX-spouse.**

If PAS goes on longer than one year…it is now called "Estrangement."

This is truly the saddest part of divorce.

The loss of a relationship because of divorce and alienation is the most devastating part of divorce. There are times when it is temporary. We all need space and time to breathe during times of conflict. But if it is chronic and consistent, you better prepare yourself for estrangement. Estrangement takes many forms and lengths. It can be healed with patience and non-attachment.

I advise you to live your life with integrity, honestly and extreme self-care.

Some day when you are going about your business, the day might come that one or all of your children may realize that you are not all that bad, that no one killed anyone and that you really did the very best you could at the time considering the circumstances and come around. NEVER expect your relationship to be what it once was or what you want it to be. Take it for what it is. Be grateful for small pieces of communication and connection. Let go of any desire to recreate the past and redefine the past.

They will have their reality and you will have yours.

It's time to make your relationship with their future. IF that is possible, then count your blessings and if it is not…know in your heart, you gave it your all and did your very best at the time to love and be loved unconditionally.

We all must deal with pain and disappointment on our own terms. It is not your children's responsibility to heal you and it is not your responsibility to heal your children. We all need to take responsibility for our own emotions and decisions.

Pray, they will see you as a fully evolved loving human and show then your grace and love for them, yourself and all of humanity as a way toward moving forward.

How to rectify… don't lose hope because children mature and know who their parents are. They will love someone on their terms and when they are ready. You cannot and should not force anyone, including your children, to "LOVE" you on your terms. Your EX will have to live with the results of their actions and so will you.

I highly suggest you watch all these amazing Documentaries: "Erased", "Split", "Marriage Story."

Well…this is a tough topic, BUT one that cannot and should not ever be overlooked when it comes to divorce. I wish PAS on NO ONE. If you experience it …you are so much more prepared…and if you do not…consider yourself one of the blessed, lucky ones. Congratulations! We have completed lesson six in chapter six.

It's time to step back and let it all simmer.

REVIEW

KIDS COME FIRST

This is an emotional subject and one never to be overlooked or set aside for later. The impact is much too great.

Follow Rosalind Sedacca's expert advice and make your divorce as child-centered as you possibly can.

Setting aside the deal-breakers of abuse or neglect, the children's relationship with BOTH parents matters.

Journal on these thoughts for your parenting plan

1. Does your parenting plan take into consideration the benefits of both parents' work schedules?
2. Driving distance between homes?
3. Do either of the parents travel for work?
4. Does it take into consideration the schedules and needs of the children? Their ages? Does it foster a strong bond?
5. Does it allow for ways to communicate respectfully?
6. Does it account for school vacations, summer vacation, holidays, Father's Day, Mother's Day, birthdays and special occasions?

It's essential to understand the reason child support is mandated... to support the children and their needs and not to be used to pay either parents expenses outside of the children's needs. This is a major reason divorced parents get into arguments. Keep receipts and know what your child's expenses are. Child Support is for the children and Spousal Support is for the spouse to get back on their feet and regain the financial footing for education, housing, etc. Alimony is no longer a given.

Each marriage is unique…length of marriage, contribution to the marriage, etc., but the laws have changed since 2018. Alimony is no longer tax deductible for the payer, and it is not taxable for the recipient. This can be a much harder sell now that things have changed. It's important to consider options and a financial buyout instead of alimony, if possible. As challenging at PAS is, we tackled it and met the possibility with grace.

Remember, knowledge is power. Your future is yours to create.

It's time to step out of the divorce story and step into creating the NEW future life you desire and deserve. You can start over. You can recreate your life the way you truly want it to be.

We are wrapping up this section of the course…and it's time to shift our work to the after.

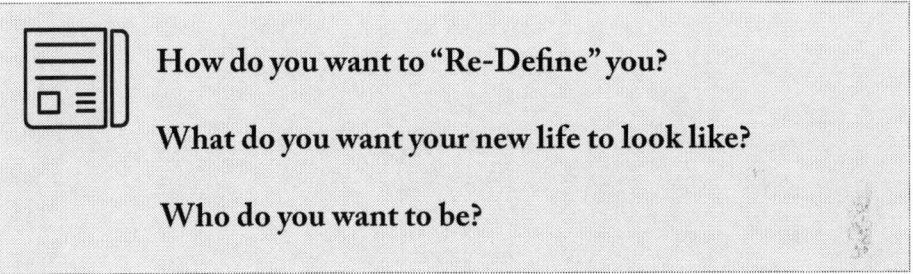

How do you want to "Re-Define" you?

What do you want your new life to look like?

Who do you want to be?

The "divorce story" begins and ends with you. That means that there is a lot of change ahead and change isn't easy. We get stuck in the past. We get stuck in our habits. We get stuck in our routines. We get stuck in our patterns. We get stuck in what others think of us or what we believe we are expected and obligated to do. We get caught up in making decisions to please only others living in our fear of rejection, judgment and disregard. These fears are real.

People may reject you. People may judge you. People may disregard you. You will be ok and so much stronger.

Living your life on your terms and not on others makes other people feel "unsafe" and "uncomfortable," and that is okay.

You deserve to be treated fairly and with respect and honesty. You deserve to be accepted and loved for exactly who you are and not as they want you to be. If your relationships are only based on what you can do for them and supplying them with what they need only to brush you aside...you don't need that relationship to be whole. It's time to let go.

If they truly care about you and love you, they will understand your need to be authentic and live a life true to yourself and they will stick around to help you, support you, cheer you on and celebrate with you on the other side. They are excited to see your new life and want to witness the journey and transformation.

Those who leave you, judge you, disregard you, pretend you don't exist and "unfriend" or "un-relative" you .... never deserve to be a part of your life to begin with...YES, that goes for family too.

You can learn to embrace your life, forgive your past, honor your heart and create a regret-free future of curiosity, growth and happiness.

Do you want to honor your heart's own song? Want to live an inspired life free of regret?

Many people suppress their feelings to keep peace with others. As a result, they tend to settle for a blah, mediocre existence and never become who they are truly capable of being.

This shouldn't be your future. Please don't let it be. You have come too far to turn back and get stuck in your story.

Remember: Bronnie Ware wrote a book called *The Top 5 Regrets of the Dying*. It's a must-read!!

1. I wish I had the courage to live a life true to myself, not the life others expected of me.
2. I wish I hadn't worked so hard.
3. I wish I'd had the courage to express my feelings.
4. I wish I had stayed in touch with my friends.
5. I wish I had let myself be happier.

Happiness IS A CHOICE. I understand how "the unknown" is both scary and exciting. Your body and mind don't know the difference. You got this and I have your back. Are you ready?

7

Redefining Self: Who Do You Want To Be?

THE FUTURE IS YOURS TO CREATE

First, we will **tackle a few tools** to step out of your old story and stop the spinning wheel of worry and obsessing about the past.

Now that the process of the divorce is finally winding down or even better yet…OVER. Now what?

Firstly, congratulations for making it this far in the journey. Celebrate your persistence, patience and courage to get through it this far. Now is when the magic really happens.

We will revisit the pathway to peace.

Then we will notice where you were and where you are now.

And ask yourself, what is the elephant that is still in the room? What issues, habits, patterns and people are we hanging on to that no longer serve us?

We have to **eliminate and discriminate** throughout the entire process of divorce.

How do we learn NOT to repeat the same old patterns that hold us back and grab us down?

We will take some time to notice our **disruptors and distractors**.

And lastly, we will take a closer look at the Top Five Regrets of the Dying to see where you stand with them to be sure the word REGRET is not in your vocabulary.

Are you ready? This is the good stuff… see you in Lesson One.

Lesson One
Step Off the Spinning Wheel

 **Get out your Journal…it's time to dig a little deeper.**

1. How do you move on with your life when your mind is racing about the past?
2. How can you step onto a new path when all you see are roadblocks?
3. It's time to train your mind to LET GO.
4. You can't heal if you are still spinning your wheels and replaying your old story repeatedly.

Here's how you start. I know this sounds a tad bizarre.

YOGA NIDRA is your answer. No, you don't have to wear yoga pants or sweat in a studio with a bunch of people chanting or bend or fold your body in odd shapes, (unless you want to try).

Yoga Nidra is Conscious sleep: your body is at rest, yet your mind accesses all brainwaves. Sleep with awareness. A state that is like the intersection of the height of mediation and sleep weaved together.

Somehow this miracle sleep can allow us to let go, moving us out of our waking consciousness and into the deepest state of rest. Yoga Nidra allows us to enter the vast, limitless state of letting go.

It is a state of hovering where we no longer cling or attach.
The state is not so far away from us…it's like a fish swimming in water.
All we must do is relax our perception to experience it.

Yoga Nidra is the access to deep relaxation, dreamless sleep and transcendent thinking.

What are the particular healing effects of transcending thinking?

Wouldn't it be incredibly helpful to shut your mind off and lessen your attachment to your thoughts?

The healing effects are quite profound and encompass three normative states ...

1. Waking
2. Dreaming
3. Sleeping

This experience allows us to **tap into the field of limitless awareness**. We have an altogether different view of ourselves. We start to objectify the vastness of which we are apart.

1. **Stage one**: become aware of the sounds in our environment and slowly bring that awareness closer and closer to you.
2. **Stage two**: bring awareness to the physical body and all its sensations. Let go of that and continue to draw that awareness inward. Shift away from sympathy.

You are no longer holding yourself, but you are being held. The more you let go, the more you are supported. No longer the doer but the witness. You are aware of the body breathing. You are not the breather.

You are not the thinker. You are aware of the mind thinking.

Put yourself to sleep while becoming increasingly effortless. Moving toward an increased state of effortlessness.

3. **Stage three**: follow or shape the breath. Reducing the amount of breath in the chest. Breathing shifts from the chest to the abdomen.

The one who is always at rest is aware. (our soul)

Non-REM sleep is the most regenerative sleep. DREAM sleep.

Pruning the memories that are no longer helpful. The complexity of our dreams.

Our soul does not go to sleep. Our body is resting, and our soul can access our deepest state of consciousness.

Non-REM stage 3 sleep: is being in a state of homeostasis.

Yoga Nidra is as close to being in a state of absolute stillness as we can get both in body, breath and mind. It is the most regenerative rest and sleep possible.

Only about 20% of our sleep is in the state of rest. Over 8 hours... we are only there for about 100 minutes.

Use of guided visualization is also used at the end. It is an image of our own making.
You reflect on the diseased state and allow the disease to drop away.

Create an intention for the healing image to come to awareness. Rest in this image for a matter of minutes: this image shifts and speeds our healing process.

How we relate to our own disease state changes too.

Summary of experience of Yoga Nidra.

- Drop into that deep state of heightened awareness while the body is at rest.
- You have an image of the problem
- You become naturally more self-aware of the problem
- You go to or through the pain or the problem

- Access a deeper unveiling of truth of you, joy that awaits the healing and consciousness at a deeper level
- When you go through the pain or the illness, you can then create a new image, a healing image that then pervades.
- Like the petals of a flower opening
- That then allows …the body to be
- Steeped in consciousness
- That can actually erase the memory of the cells that function negatively.

I recommend you download the APP "Sanctuary" with Rod Stryker and engage in Yoga Nidra at least 3 times per week. Set aside 20 minutes per session.

Yoga Nidra takes NO skill…just a commitment to practice the deepest state of rest coupled with awareness. It's contagious and it is so healing.

Learning to let go is easier when you practice regularly.

I want to shift our focus now to keeping a journal. I have suggested you keep a planner, calendar, goal setting and journal during all the stages of divorce, **BUT now I am referring to a journal that allows you to step out of your story and access the future life you truly desire.**

 **It's time to access and trust the voice of your soul.**

The best way to access the voice of the soul is to write, write, write.

Use a digital journal if you are truly concerned about your privacy… but I do highly suggest the written word instead. Write every day. Write anytime you feel stuck or confused. Write, write, write…and do not worry about what you write about, how long you write for, spelling, grammar, etc. ... none of it matters.

Just write.

The beautiful healing words you write will bring such clarity and peace to your heart and soul. AND if you are angry, hurt or frustrated...no one needs to get yelled at .... just write about it. Share your feelings with pen and paper and let it all out. Learn to let go on paper. It's safe and healthy. You can always burn it and create a new one. Keep it SAFE. Never share where you keep it or what you write. This is your sacred space.

I also suggest you revisit the **practice of sitting in silence for 5-10 minutes every morning** when you awake. Practicing the art of mindful meditation is a skill you will never regret having. Mindful meditation is a healing practice and a form of meditation or induced relaxation that focuses awareness on breathing and encourages positive attitudes to achieve a healthy, balanced mental state.

If you need a hand to hold or you want guidance ... download the **APP Sanctuary** for your mediation too...OR **try the CALM app.** Honestly there are SO many meditation apps. There is no excuse not to try one...and most of them have free trials or are free altogether. Sit in silence and watch the body breathing. Be careful, slow, deliberate and aware of the body breathing and fill your heart with love and gratitude for all the gifts and blessings you do have. Focus on the positive and visualize the body relaxed and healthy in mind, body and spirit.

Oxygen is life. **Breath is how we maintain our life.**

IN yoga, we call it PRANA. Breath Work > Practice living in the NOW. Pulling fresh oxygen into the body to reoxygenate our blood and pushing stale old air out of the body is stepping up your game to living a life in alignment with your greatest sense of wellness.

See the connection of the body to the breath to the mind. Our breath is the bridge to our wellness.

I was never much of a Law of Attraction kind of girl until I met Taylor Wells.

She is my soul sister and we don't have to say much to know what the other is thinking. Taylor is an eternal optimist. She knows my story. I know hers. We share our sacred space, show up and love each other no matter what from a place of the law of attraction. The Law of Attraction is simple. You attract what you put out there.

The law of attraction means being able to attract whatever one wants in life by focusing one's mind's eye on what one wants, whether positive or negative. In philosophy, the belief is based on the principle that humans are made of energy, likewise their thoughts. We are nothing but energy.

Ever notice how some people and places have positive energy?
Ever notice how some people and places have negative energy?

What are you emitting?
What is your home saying about you?
What are your thoughts saying about you?
What are your friends saying about you?
What are you saying about you?
Let your actions and habits do the speaking.

There are no mistakes...ONLY Lessons.
The brain hears your negative thinking.
The mind knows what you are putting out there negatively.
If you have a negative thought...own it...acknowledge it and change it to a positive one.
No need to make a big deal about it.

Just up level your thinking.

This is when we all need a coach. We all need a cheerleader, an advocate and a guide to support us when we are exhausted and guide us when we are lost.

We aren't afraid of hiring a sports coach for our kids. We have no fear of having a trainer at the gym, BUT when it comes to our life …we just brush it aside and let it all go. It's no use. I don't deserve anything better than what I have.
It's as good as it's even going to get.
It's too this. It's too that.

Healing and transforming from divorce is no joke. This is precisely the time you need a coach to help guide, support, encourage, inspire, empower and love you.

But not a friend who will listen to your lies and bullshit and excuses …etc.

I am an expert coach who has the skills and wisdom, the experience and resources, to get you to where you want to go. Determine what area of your life needs the most help and support and do a bit of research to find a qualified coach. I wish I had!

Lesson Two is coming up next as we work on reconnecting and re-evaluating our family and friends.

NOTES

LESSON TWO

RE-CONNECT AND RE-EVALUATE

 **The next step is to reevaluate your past life to prepare for your future life.**

1. Which relationships do you need to keep?
2. Which relationships make you smile?
3. Which relationships can you and do you feel good about?
4. Which relationships are contributing to you being a better, more productive person?
5. Which relationships are in alignment with your values?
6. Which relationships are reciprocal?
7. Which relationships are fun and loving?

Make a list and write down how each person makes you feel and how they contribute to your life.
Now, it's time to do the same for the people in your life that don't do any of these things for you.

These are negative, hurtful, use you, lie to you, gossip about you, make you sad, you hide your feelings from them, you fear them, you dislike them for whatever reason, you avoid or hide from them. I could keep going but you see the pattern.

Yes, people aren't all good or all bad. But you know in your heart if someone is good for you OR they are not good for you. You now have the right and the responsibility to yourself and your children to let go of anything and anyone that is not serving your best and highest good.

Did you make your list of Family and Friends? Who to keep and who to let go of?

 **I suggest you create lists of people from different areas of your life.**

1. Family
2. Extended Family
3. Old friends
4. New friends
5. Work/Peers
6. Professionals
7. Neighbors
8. Anyone else that sticks around

What habits and patterns need to be reevaluated?

Do you have negative habits or patterns because of the people you associate with? Perhaps you need to let go of both the habit and the friend? Now you might think I am cruel. I understand. You have some critical decisions to make.

Ask yourself…If I had to do it all over again, would I choose this person to be in my life? What are the emotions you are feeling about having OR not having this person or situation in your life anymore?

- Relief?
- Sadness?
- Joy?
- Surrender?
- Blessed?

Now it's time to reconnect and reevaluate to your budget and your relationship with money. How is your relationship with your money? Is it a positive relationship? Is it a negative relationship?

Do you speak the same language? Does your relationship align with your values and goals?

Keep a MONEY journal for 60 days to identify your relationship with money.

- Do you use money, or does money use you?
- Do you take money for granted?
- Do you hoard money? Are you stingy or cheap?
- Do you spend it needlessly or to the point of irresponsibility?
- Are you in debt? How do you feel about being in debt?
- Do you have a financial advisory that you trust and speak to regularly?
- Do people owe you money?
- Do you owe people money?

This lesson is a deep dive into a lot of sensitive issues.

Don't get angry...open your eyes and become fully aware. Lesson Three is coming your way. To see the next chapter of your life, you must Surrender and allow the new to unfold. Let's explore all the possibilities.

NOTES

LESSON THREE
EXPLORE ALL YOUR POSSIBILITIES

Have you ever given any thought to your hidden talents? Or exploring hidden talents that you never fully developed? Hint hint...you picked up the guitar but quit because you didn't have time...or your spouse told you that you didn't have the talent.

 **It is also time to revisit your old passions.**

- What did you love to do that you stopped doing when you got married or took a job or had a child or moved?
- What did you do when you were a kid that you miss doing?
- What do you like doing that you stopped doing because you felt you didn't have time for it...like cooking or decorating or traveling or reading or going to the gym or running or...the list is long, I imagine?

Write the answers to these questions in your journal. It is easier if you're journaling. Get it down on paper, so it's real and concrete and not just some random ...nahhh...I can't think of anything. Take the time to write down what you love to do. What you miss doing and what's important to you. Can you create a small corner of your house to sit still, reflect and write every day for a few minutes?

New possibilities are found in stillness.

Next, it's time to get out there!! When you know what you miss doing or always wanted to do. Research where near you other people do that, when they do it, how much it costs and if you know anyone else that likes to do that too.

If money is a concern…and it always is when you are getting divorced… **volunteer!**

Everyone needs help with something. One of the best ways to get out of your head with your problems is to help other people with theirs.

No, you are not the only one with problems and fears. You are definitely not alone. **Join a meet-up, a group** or a club. Find other like-minded people who love to do what you love to do, even if it's been 40 years! It's never too late.

Now you say to me…but Paulette, I am not a social person. I am an introvert, or a homebody and I like to do things quietly by myself. That's fine too!! Engage in an online course, commit to trying new foods, take a walk in nature, or engage in an activity you enjoy at home.

Start an online side hustle: Sell wine, make-up, essential oils, CBD products etc. You'll love the money and you will make so many new friends.

It's time to get inspired: Watch a Ted Talk, download a documentary, enroll in an adult education course.

Plenty of other people are looking to engage in fun, educational activities.

And for you extroverts…consider a group travel tour. Travel with a singles group to a location you have always wanted to go, but your ex didn't …well NOW is the time to GO. Where did you want to go? Let's make a list of locations and check on some travel deals.

Grab a friend and book a **road trip or a getaway.** You won't regret it. It's time to get excited about the future. I know you don't know what that looks like yet…but remember your future life will unfold sooner that you think. And it will happen when you are inspired by learning new things and revisiting some of our old loves you forgot about.

In lesson four we are going to work on one of my absolute favorite topics…making room for the NEW.

LESSON FOUR
MAKE ROOM FOR THE NEW

Can you start to see how exciting your new life can be ahead of you and not behind you? You may be slightly overwhelmed by all this talk about the future and how many options and choices you have. I understand.

When I moved out and sat on the floor with nothing but cardboard boxes surrounding me...all I did was cry. My life was a mess. I had no idea where I came from and I had no idea where I was going. My life was a blur and felt empty and meaningless. I felt used and confused. All I knew was I was torn, and my heart was hurting.

Yes, I was free of living in an unhappy marriage. I was free of living in constant chaos and turmoil. But I deeply missed my children and I missed having security and stability. I found the peace I longed for, but everything else was uncertain. It was indeed too much uncertainty.

I knew I needed stability and security and a routine to ground me. This is what we all need at this time. Let go of the old to make room for the new while still feeling secure and loved. Is this possible? Yes...it is.

It's time to go drawer by drawer, closet by closet, room by room, box by box and keep what feels solid and good and loving and kind and let go of anything that is holding you back from healing and practicing self-care and self-love. Now that you've explored new possibilities, it's time to deal with all your "stuff".

To whatever level YOU are comfortable with, it's time to go through everything you own and **decide what to keep and what you can let go of.**

If you do not know who Marie Kondo is...well open up your eyes and read *The Magical Art of Tidying Up*. And empty your closets and category by category, go piece by piece, item by item and ask yourself as you pick up each item "does this spark joy?" (thanks Marie Kondo www.konmari.com)) If the answer is YES!! Keep it. It is the answer if NO!! You have a decision to make. Should you sell it? Donate it? Give it away or throw it out?

You can do this room by room...but Marie says it's best to do it by category. Now I am not a Kondo certified organizer...but I have to say...I rock at it. I can help you, OR you can grab a good friend. Make a deal...they help you with your stuff, and in return, you help them with theirs.

It's an exhausting day or two ...but when you are done...it's truly heaven. You will feel ten years younger and 10 pounds lighter. The hardest things are mementos or nostalgia. Nostalgia is a way of holding on to the past and trying to recreate what is gone.

Many people hold on to remember what used to be- don't let nostalgia get in the way of your beautiful new life. Let it go. Keep ONLY those things that genuinely bring you extreme joy and make room for the new. I like to call it essentialism, not minimalism.

Keep what is essential and useful. Let go of what is clutter and stale old negative energy.

Take a picture of it if you just can't let it go. Put everything in a box, tape it up, mark it Nostalgia and if you cannot remember what is in the box one year later...you DO NOT need it. Right?

What to do with an engagement ring- have you heard of Worthy?
Many women want to sell their diamond ring…instead of remake it
into another piece of jewelry. A few reasons.

- The value is too high
- The memories are too great
- Good can be done with the money

Most jewelry stores will hardly give you what your ring is worth.
Check out www.sellring.com to see if you want to sell your ring. If it
is GIA certified and you have the paperwork, you will get a lot more
for it.

I know not everyone has an easy time decluttering. It's very emotional and very time consuming. Some people have the tendency to
hold on to everything. We see our stuff as our identity and our security. If you genuinely are overwhelmed and you want to declutter and
begin the process, I suggest you **consider hiring a home organizer!!**

**Professional home organizers make order out of chaos and change
our lives in a matter of a few days… (on average) and the cost is
truly worth every penny.** Most charge by the hour. They are diligent
and hard workers and don't waste time. You may find a few that will
estimate the amount of time it takes and give you a set rate for the
job. Room by room or full house if needed. Check out a few home
organizer's websites before and after pictures for inspiration and a
sense of relief. I get goosebumps every time I see the transformations.

I personally have done full houses, businesses, pantries, kitchens,
offices, closets, and children's playrooms.

I've seen women lose ten years off their life without all these extra
things!

And the added income from selling extra things they didn't even
remember they had was liberating.

 **What are your biggest hurdles holding you back?**

Here I go again asking you to journal your emotions and reasons for wanting to hold on.

What are you afraid of?

A "lack mentality" will come along with you into the future. Your future life will hold on to those fears.

I have seen a sense of desperation that leads to grasping, hoarding, being stuck in a rut, and rigid thinking. If this is you, please seek out help. There is so much help for you. Do not try to go it alone. There are excellent therapists out there equipped with helping people lighten the load and make room for the new.

By now, you should feel inspired to let go a little bit at a time. It won't happen overnight. Letting go is a process. The load is lighter. The path ahead is beautiful and less burdened. Your freedom is just taking flight.

OMG, it's time to start talking about dating. Are you as excited as I am??? This is going to be fun.

LESSON FIVE
DATING IN THE DIGITAL AGE

This is scary stuff…right? I can't imagine only knowing dating on-line. Is it me, or does it seem mechanical and impersonal? Sleazy and cold? Swipe right I like you. Swipe left…NO thank you.

The importance of your internet dating profile is critical. You need to come across as approachable yet professional. Attractive but not trashy. Friendly but not flighty.

Things to consider:

1. What do I wear?
2. How do I answer all these questions?
3. What do I want on a date?
4. Am I ready to date?
5. Do I want a new relationship?
6. Am I ready for a new relationship?
7. Maybe I just want sex? This is so confusing and uncomfortable.
8. Maybe I am not ready to have sex yet?

The best advice is to BE YOU. **YOU MUST KNOW WHAT YOU WANT.**

Hiring a dating and relationship coach to help you set up your pro-file is a good idea if you are nervous and tech is not your thing. Each sight has its pros and cons. Sites come and go. Do your research. If you have friends who have had success with one site…go with that.

Popular online dating sites:

- Bumble
- Hinge
- Syncd
- Zoosk
- Elite
- Eharmony
- Christian Singles
- Silver Singles (over 50)

1. If you have funds and are looking for your equal... Could Millionaire Match be for you?
2. There are a lot of sites for Sugar Daddies. No comment.
3. Now, what if you already started dating the old-fashioned way?
4. In-person, meet and greet?
5. A blind date?
6. Can I ask you for your number?

Dating opens the door to so many emotions. Trust? I am not going to go through this hell again feelings are normal.

Take it slow and steady. Getting involved too soon is NEVER a good idea.

When is it time to start dating again? If you already have...again... take it slow. If you need to take a break...take it! If you need to let go of old relationships...let go!

How to know when you are ready...only you will know. How to find a new partner...blind date, old school meeting, online. Let it happen naturally.

Who is right for you? You NEED to know what your criteria are. YOU can start over. You have the responsibility to be clear about what you want and what you need.

When someone comes on too strong and is ready to move in after three dates, it's a RED FLAG.

 **Here are a few things to think about or journal to get clear on your emotions.**

1. Sex in a new age. How does online dating feel to you?
2. NO one can tell you what is right for you. What is your gut telling you?
3. Do not fall for the first man who shows you some attention.
4. Sex is sex. Love is love.
5. What do you want? What do you need?
6. Loving too soon!
7. Too soon is usually within 6-12 months of your divorce.
8. Time is a good thing. Give it time.
9. Get to know ALL about the other person.
10. No one is perfect, but they should always be honest, kind and respectful.
11. The rest is just details.
12. When and how to introduce someone to the kids.
13. This is a tender subject.
14. If your children are ages 3-18, there is NO need to introduce your children to anyone you are dating.
15. Children only need to be kindly introduced to your new partner after you have been dating seriously for at least six months and you are out on your own.
16. I suggest a casual lunch or outdoor event where the kids are the main focus, i.e., a Carnival, a BBQ, a music event. Not in your home or a formal dinner or family event.
17. Introduce your date as a new person you enjoy spending time with. If they are a special person and they treat you well, your children will pick up on that and most will be happy that you are happy even if it means that there is NO chance mom and dad will ever get back together again.
18. Many children secretly pray their parents still love each other and will work it out.

19. When someone new enters the picture…those dreams are shattered. Some children are sad. Some are happy. Most are confused but want you to be happy. Don't pressure them to like your new date.
20. Just be there to answer questions and reassure them you love them, and they always come first.
21. If you are the primary custody parent, it may be difficult for your new partner to "move-in" for many reasons.

   a. Privacy
   b. Child support
   c. Alimony
   d. Rumors
   e. Hurt feelings
   f. Parenting conflicts
   g. Your Ex's anger and jealousy

I advise you and your new partner to be very sensitive to these emotions. Give it plenty of time and wait until the children are out of the house, or there is an engagement. The ages of the children will determine a lot of these sensitive topics. These are many of the issues I work through with my divorce coaching clients. Also, a lot depends on who is paying the bills, and if your new partner has children of their own. The key here is SLOW.
Talk it out with kindness and sensitivity.

And what do you do if they move in and it doesn't work out?
How do you let go when it's not going well?
How do you ask them to move out?

With honesty, sensitivity and love.

Your life is your life.
YOU do not want to go through another divorce again.
YOU are going to live your life on your terms.

YOU are going to practice extreme self-care and lead with love in all your actions.

Agree? You can see how dating properly can set you up for success or failure.

And lastly …

How to deal with the pressure and opinions of family and friends. Perhaps they have vast knowledge or insight…listen and absorb their words.

Listen with love, thank them for "caring," and let it go. They are not in control of your future. Lead with love. You must be in control of your future. No one is in control of your future, but you!

If dating isn't right for you yet…don't consider it. The time will come when you know you are ready.
Now it's time to consider adding a bit of adventure into your new life.

LESSON SIX
ADVENTURES IN FREEDOM

There are so many ways to learn to smile again. Are you ready to explore them?

Adventure is defined as an unusual and exciting, typically hazardous, experience or activity.

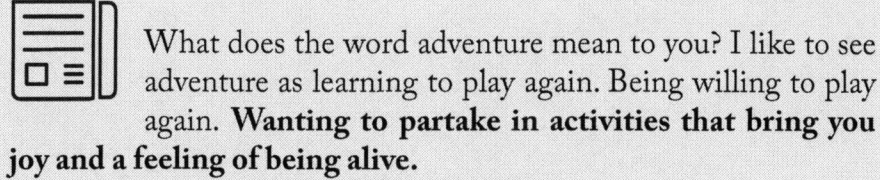 What does the word adventure mean to you? I like to see adventure as learning to play again. Being willing to play again. **Wanting to partake in activities that bring you joy and a feeling of being alive.**

1. What does adventure mean to you?
2. Where do you want to go?
3. Who do you want to meet?
4. Why do you want to go there?
5. Do you want to go alone or bring someone with you?

Let's explore what makes you giddy? Silly? Laugh? Forget who you think you are? What people think of you? What makes you want to raise the bar and ask for more? Expect more? What makes you want to challenge yourself and take risks?

No, not crazy dangerous risks…well maybe just a few.

Get out your journal and write, write, write!

 Okay …now tell me? What makes you excited? How do you find joy? Is it travel? Rest? What makes you feel most alive? Can you finally give yourself permission to live life on your own terms and for no one else's agenda?

 **Grab your journal again and let's create your bucket list.** How about we start with 50 things you want to do before 50? Or 60 things you want to do before 60? Whatever your age is…add ten years and get writing!

REVIEW

THE FUTURE IS YOURS

I told you this chapter was a game-changer. I am so proud of you for gearing up to explore and create the next amazing chapter of your life. By now, you must realize that the future is yours to create, to live and to explore.

Yes, life is an adventure and you deserve to live it all to the fullest with no regrets. Let's recap a few highlights.

What are the benefits of Yoga Nidra and Meditation?

Please notice anytime you need to press pause and reevaluate anything that you are doing that doesn't feel quite right. You can stop and let it simmer and digest a bit before you move on.

Did you learn what inspires you most? Write down those inspirations and post them anywhere you can read them repeatedly.

What did you make room for? What did you learn to let go of? How does it feel to only have what sparks joy?

Did you see a clear picture of what dating in the digital age may look like for you? What site might you use?

What kind of relationship are you looking for? How are you going to protect yourself online?

I'm all ears… Share with me three things that are on your bucket list! Email me them NOW. I really want to know.

I know…I seem a bit more excited about your future than you do…
but I'm like that. Now it's your turn. Share with me all your break-
throughs. And finally, and I do mean finally, you can rejoice, you are
ready for Chapter Eight.

Take time for your Life! See you in our final module together.

NOTES

8

KNOW YOURSELF

TAKE TIME FOR YOUR LIFE

Well, you did the work. I just held your hand. Please take a moment to give yourself some praise for taking on this journey with me. This is and will be the most challenging and most rewarding accomplishment you have ever had to live through…surviving and thriving through divorce. The next step is the future is yours for the taking.

It's time to truly know thyself.

I had no idea who I was until the age of 50. I sold, gave away and packed literally everything left I owned into a truck on its way to Belize. I left all that I knew and let go of the old to create a new life full of adventure, self-love and unconditional devotion to a love that found me and saved me. I got remarried, moved to an agrihood, started several new businesses, let go of toxic relationships and committed to living my best life that I would NEVER have seemed possible if I didn't take the time and do the work.

You see, I was trapped in a life that wasn't mine to live. I lived in a life that was chosen for me and I quietly went along for the ride until I finally hit a bottom that was so painful, I contemplated suicide continuously for months. I wanted out of the pain I had, living a life to make other people happy and to take care of them regardless of the damage it did to my body and soul. I don't want that for you. I ask you to do the work now.

Know thyself and live your fullest best life ever. The future is beautiful when you live it right. We finally approach this last module in this course we share together.

*Of all the chapters, this one will **prepare you and set you up for success in your life ahead**. So, listen up! And get your journal ready. We will address how to create a robust financial future. The decision you will have to make* *about returning to your maiden name, keeping your married name or a combination of the two.*

We will explore The Four Desires in creating your own unique dharma code, your personal goals and the sabotaging habits you may still be holding onto. How to prioritize yourself in the process of dating all while committing yourself to the mindset that new love is possible.

There is a bit of divorce recovery work ahead and the power of the healing work yet to come. And finally, the excitement ahead as you learn to celebrate every success and tiny win you have ahead of you.

LESSON ONE
CREATE A FINANCIAL FUTURE

It's now time to explore the need to create a financial future that will give you safety and security.

Is it hard to believe you are ready to start your new life? This is a wonderful thing...but it is also a big responsibility. You have no one to tell you what to do or be in control of your decisions and choices, BUT that also means **you are now responsible for your decision and your choices**.

The first thing you must secure is to update all your accounts. New login and new passwords. Even if you did that when the paperwork was filed it's time to update it again. Update your name, new address, new email and maybe even a new phone number.

This is the beginning of your new life on your terms. **It starts with your finances**.

Do everything you can to pay off all debt. You want to create a fresh start with a clean slate. Debt is a killer. It's best to consult with a financial expert to pay off your debt and secure a stronger beginning.

It's time also to **update insurance policies** to reflect your new life. Taking out a life insurance policy on your ex to secure your financial future is a consideration.

If you have not already done so...**close all joint credit card** accounts, **remove ex-spouse name from all remaining accounts,** and go through all of your financials carefully to be sure you are protected from any future debt on their part.

Also, **keep copies of your certified divorce decree** to prove any future income or release of financial claim or responsibility.

If your financials are complicated, be sure to **find a qualified financial planner.**

A Certified Divorce Financial Planner is highly suggested. Also, choose one that is well aware of your income needs, tax ramifications and your risk tolerance. Are you a conservative investor? Are you a risk-taker?

Be sure you are on the same page with your advisor. If they are really a stock manager who makes commissions on trades and your idea of investing in a secure pension...you are setting yourself up for failure.

Your next step is to be certain the **transfer of all ownership of any property**, accounts and assets have been properly done. Deeds, titles and accounts transfers can sometimes fall through the cracks.

After you are all set up with the paperwork, it is time to create an estate plan.

Estate plans are not terribly complicated, but they do take some consideration and time to create.

An attorney that specializes in Estate Planning and Wills is best, but if you know all of your financials are properly assigned to beneficiaries, you should be in good shape.

 **Things to consider.**

1. Who will pay your debts after you die? (The goal is to have no debt)
2. Who will pay for your burial or cremation?
3. Who will inherit your assets? How will they be distributed?

This can be very emotional. It's not easy to consider yourself dead and how life will be for the people you love that you leave behind. It is not your responsibility to make their life comfortable. You have the right to do what you want with your assets. Do what you want with your money. Leave it to who you want. But I suggest you don't try to control people from your grave. Let it go.

Leave it with love, OR don't leave it at all. Find a way to leave what you want to who you love and allow them to remember you with love and respect…not fear and anger.

If you have financially irresponsible people in your life …yes, it is wise to have an executor to oversee a sense of reason and responsibility but not out of spite or control.

Now it's time to create a budget you can stick with!! Be consistent in your spending and savings.

Your budget needs to reflect your new values and lifestyle. What are your priorities?

Protecting credit is very important now. I want you to **update and check in on your credit report routinely**. If you see any discrepancies call each credit agency and dispute them.

Financial Advisement is an ongoing process. Stay in touch with your expert.

Establishing a relationship with a financial advisor that will look after you, but won't try to sell you financial options you don't fully understand is recommended.

**Consider setting up a private pension fund for your retirement.
Consider a Home Equity Conversion Mortgage Purchase if you or your spouse is over 62.
Consider taking out a life insurance policy on your ex or your parents.**

These are not easy fixes. It takes time and a commitment to secure your future and your credit if you stay on top of it. Once your finances are in shape, the rest will fall into place.

Speaking of changes. It's time to decide if you want to change your name.

Lesson Two
To name change or not to name change?

This is a very personal choice. It is never an easy decision if you have children under the age of 18. It simply makes it easier to travel, attend events, deposit or withdraw money for your children, hear from school administrators and sports coaches etc., if your name is the same as your children. BUT it also means that you also will carry with you the label and stigma of being included in that "family" of names.

 **Let's journal on name changing**

- Is that something you are willing to hold on to?
- Is that something you are ready to let go of?
- Is that important to you?
- What is the advantage in your eyes to keeping your old name?
- What is the advantage of letting go of your old name?
- What is the new name you want to return to?

Take some time to decide what name you want to carry forward with you. This decision will affect every document moving forward.

I decided to hold onto my married name until my youngest turned 21. You will need to make your own decision.
A name is just a name…but changing it is a lot of work and expense.

Now that I look back at it, I was still holding on to what I hoped for…cooperation and respect.

My ex filed a motion for the judge to have me "recused" from using it. The judge denied him. He said and I quote, "In 16 years on the bench, I have never seen a request for such a demand".

Keep OR take whatever name you desire... but know some may object and judge you.

IF you change your name, some will see you as rejecting your children. IF you keep your name, some will see you as controlling. Once you decide whether to keep your married name or go back to your birth name...there are a few things to consider.

You have the choice of variations. Changing your name will be costly and time-consuming. **Your decision impacts ALL documents.**

- Social security number
- Driver's license
- Passport
- Global entry
- Financial accounts
- Credit cards
- Mortgage
- Deeds and titles
- Insurance
- Wills

And just about everything else your name is on!!

Take your time to decide what is best for you.
Can you make changes in stages? How many years until your children are of age? Is it worth the hassle?
This is a very personal decision, BUT one to consider wisely.

Now you are ready for Lesson Three.
Creating a goal-setting mind map that will secure your future happiness and success.

LESSON THREE
GOAL SETTING

You are well on your way to securing your future. Now it is time to concentrate on "Goal Setting" to set up your future self for success!!

It may seem obvious to have goals...right? I mean... who doesn't have goals?

But goals are not achieved if you are not able to identify them clearly and have benchmarks along the way to keep you on target and with incentives and rewards coming your way when you reach a goal.

Think about anything you have ever achieved.

How did you feel when you achieved it?
How did it change your attitude about yourself?
How did that affect your momentum and commitment to keep moving through the tough spots of other goals you have but are still working on? You know the feeling...right?

 **Let's recall a time in your life when you nailed a goal.**

- What was the goal?
- When was it?
- Where were you?
- How did it make you feel?

You may be new to the concept of mind mapping. I was. I was introduced to mind mapping while at Kripalu in the Berkshires of Massachusetts, celebrating my birthday, in the summer of 2011. I was lucky enough to be introduced to Rod Stryker, who wrote the book *The Four Desires*. Nine years later, since 2012, I have been using, teaching and coaching *The Four Desires* or what Rod calls the yoga of fulfillment. In the book, Rod describes a technique that is instrumental in accessing the subconscious mind and the voice of your deepest driving desires. Mind Mapping has been credited to several psychologists...**particularly Tony Buzon**.

I can't imagine creating such a tool. All I know is that it works.

Allowing myself to release my attachment to the outcome and access a deeper layer of your awareness changed my life.

I had no idea that my mind, heart and soul could be accessed and utilized collectively. Being a witness of such a process, I know it is true and authentic.

The process for Mind Mapping is as follows:

Grab some colored pens. You can work in your journal or on blank unlined paper
Step 1. Turn paper to landscape position
Step 2. Draw a picture in the middle that represents your main idea.
Step 3. Draw some thick lines coming from the middle picture. This is for each of the main ideas.
Step 4. Draw pictures where possible.
Step 5. From each of the thicker lines, draw thinner connected lines spreading out like the branches of a tree. These are for other ideas.

All writing should be KEY words only. Keep your words printed in CAPITAL letters.

Each branch should have its own color. Keep adding new ideas!!

Experiment with the process and outcome.

There are three main parts of this work.

1. Dharma Code (a mission statement OR what I like to call the visionary statement of your soul)
2. Sankalpa: your short-term goal OR resolution that you can achieve within 6-18 months.
3. Vikalpa: your sabotaging behavior that always throws you off track from your desired outcome.

I cannot advise you enough to read the book *The Four Desires* by Rod Stryker. The book and his teachings will change your life. They changed mine. So much so Rod Stryker was the officiate when my new husband and I married on August 28th, 2017.

Vision creates results in all possibilities.

 **Let's celebrate each other's loves and passions!!** What does that look like for you? Here are some thoughts to get you started:

1. Moving?
2. Work?
3. Service?
4. Dreams?
5. Relationships?
6. Freedom?

IF you lived your life in alignment with your passions and your patience, what would your life look like? How would it be different? This is a deep topic that needs to be addressed. Do NOT overlook this stage.

You are almost there, and you can do it. Let's celebrate each other's loves and passions!!

This lesson is very deep and SHOULD require personal coaching. Read over the protocol and prompts and decide what it is that you need.

In lesson four, we challenge the lesson that new love is possible, just like it was for me and all of my clients. Yes, all!

LESSON FOUR
NEW LOVE IS POSSIBLE

New love is possible! Is that what you want?

New love happens after you heal and fall back in love with yourself. This takes time and the amount of time is different for everyone. You need to fall back in love with yourself **first** and become a stronger, better version of yourself.

When you least expect it, and when you are ready, the universe gives you what you put out. The universe will give you what you need only after you have done the work. Are you willing to staying open to all possibilities?

We talked about dating. Keep your eyes wide open! Learn to trust your instincts again.

Although the statistics are not good: 50% of 2nd; 75% of 3rd marriages end in divorce.

- Be aware of repeating old patterns:
- If you did in the past, do not take on someone else's grief or negativity.
- Do not take on a project.
- Do not take on a wounded soul.
- Do not take on a charity case.
- Do not take on a narcissist.

Remember the behaviors of narcissists.
- Love Bombing.
- Gaslighting.
- Control.

- Jealousy.
- Manipulating
- Lack of empathy
- Passive-aggressive
- Invalidating
- Scapegoating
- Future faking
- Mirroring
- Baiting
- Use of flying monkeys
- Breadcrumbing
- Devaluing
- Triangulating
- Ghosting
- Projecting

For starters, …these are the usual signs, to begin with.

If you feel out of control… and you feel confused and as if you are walking on eggshells, you are probably dating a narcissist.

Get help! Don't go it alone.

Communication is everything.

How do you fine-tune those skills?
How do you learn to be 100% responsible for yourself?
How to take control of your life?
Your future? Your destiny?

Your future is yours to create.

A partner will compliment you, but they won't complete you.
When you are doing the work on your healing, your career, your relationships, your boundaries, your education, your service, your community and your self-care…love comes.

Self-love and self-care breed universal love.

In Lesson Five, we are going to dig deep into the healing process, because it's just that - a process.

THE POWER OF HEALING

When your divorce is over and the ink is dry, this is when the journey really begins.

It begins with you consciously and carefully crafting and creating your new life you deserve and desire. Let's explore ways to facilitate healing.

In my opinion, it begins with experiencing the practice of GRACE.

Can you continue to find grace in every day? How can we explore finding grace in the everyday? The work of my friend and expert coach Anne Jolles walks us through the process brilliantly. She wrote and developed a practice called walking the **Grace Trails**. You can listen to my "Thriving in Chaos" Podcast to hear her explain more. https://anchor.fm/dashboard/episode/e4h7bb

 **It's a process of being aware of each of these five steps:**

GRACE: Gratefulness, Release, Acceptance, Challenge, Embrace

Gratefulness:
Each day when you awaken, take a moment to begin with a sense of all that you have to be grateful for. What is going well in your life? What do you have to be grateful for? There is always something to be grateful for.

Truly soak in the essence of being alive.
The feeling of a long hot shower.

The warmth of the sun on your face.
A full refrigerator, a soft warm bed, your adoring pet, a cool glass
of clean water.
A delicious, simple meal.

The simple things are often overlooked. All things that so many of us take for granted.

Release:
Take a moment to contemplate what it is you need to release from your life, your home, your soul, your heart. What is weighing heavy on you? What are you holding on to that is no longer serving you? What is a habit that is holding you back from being your best self? What fears and thoughts can you release? It's important to peel away and let go as much as it is to receive.

Acceptance:
Take a moment to contemplate what it is that you need to accept as the truth. What is a fact that you have been hoping would change for a very long time that is out of your control? Who do you believe won't change (patterns) that you need to accept as fact? What do you need to acknowledge about the past or present that will allow you to move beyond wishing, hoping, begging, pleading will change that won't? Acceptance is liberating. Give it a try and continue to keep peeling away the layers every day of things, people, situations and habits that no longer serve you.

Challenge:
Take a moment to contemplate how you need to challenge yourself to grow, learn, shift, expand, improve and understand yourself and your goals better? Do you need to enroll in a course? Do you need to stop or end something? Do you need to go back to get a degree? Do you need to lose weight? Establish an exercise routine again? Change your diet? Take better care of yourself? Spend less and save more? Get a better job? It's time to take stock in how you need

to take steps in challenging yourself to create lasting change and improve your lifestyle.

Embrace:
And finally, take a moment to embrace the moment. We only have the moment you are currently residing in. Don't rush it or wish it away. Embrace the totality of each moment. Stop to look around and notice the details.

If this topic excites you …but feels a bit of a challenge. I suggest you read *The Power of Now* by Eckhart Tolle.
Learning to embrace life as it is given to us will begin your healing faster.

You can also take five stepping stones and place them in your front or back yard, or you can create a banner with each of the five steps on it in a place you see every day to remind you of living in a state of grace and walking your own GRACE Trail.

Anne's magic trail inspires me to know I truly am in control of creating my life. Yes, there are things out of my control, but I am in control of my reactions to them.

Going even deeper, I recommend the healing work of the late great Louise Hay. I had the pleasure of meeting her in June 2012 in New York City at The Hay House Writings' Workshop. I was at the beginning of my journey deciding to write my memoir and her inspiration stays with me every day. She recreated her life at the age of 60 when she began her publishing company Hay House. If you are ever in need of some inspiration and clarity, turn to her excellent work.

In my opinion, her book *You Can Heal Your Life* is life-changing. It taught me that our thoughts are our reality. What you believe to be true will manifest not only in our thoughts, but in our bodies, as ailments if not dealt with, healed and released, they will manifest themselves in our lives as a disease.

As a child, I was taught that children were to be seen and not heard. My sisters moved out when I was very young (they were much older) and I never spoke honestly to them. They ignored me and I ignored them.
My parents were disconnected and didn't speak honestly to each other. They wore a mask and I learned to stay quiet and co-depend. My family lived a pretend life of "the show must go on." I was pleasant and agreeable. I was cooperative and stayed around to take care of my parents. I had desires but didn't share them or pursue them. It was easier just to be pleasant than combative. I remained quiet until I could no longer endure suffering in silence.

It got worse when I married. What I learned and continued to pretend was that I was Cinderella and he was Prince Charming. It slowly took its toll on me. I developed an underbite, ground my teeth, and had recurring strep throat. I had braces for four years that gave me horrible canker sores, which also contributed to me not smiling and keeping quiet. In my 30's, I developed nodules on my vocal cords and suffered extreme ear pain, with a dysfunctional Eustachian tube, TMJ and a severe case of Tinnitus. All from my keeping my mouth shut, holding my tongue, not speaking my truth and pretending I was "fine."

It wasn't until I read Louise Hay's book that I understood the manifestation of my emotional pains to physical ailments and pain. I also learned that the Left side of the body is Female, and the Right side of the body is Male.
If your left side is giving you trouble, it's usually a female that is doing you harm. And so, with the right and a male.

Louise teaches us how to do "Mirror Work": This may seem and feel a bit odd to do, BUT it's worth a try.
Look at yourself in the mirror and say to yourself, "Louise (insert your name) …I really love you. Or I really approve of you. Or I really

accept and unconditionally love you. OR respect…OR whatever it is that you find struggling." Louise makes the case that mirror work is a rewire of the messages that you have been taught as a child (and adult) that are abusive, critical and damaging. This is NOT narcissism. Healing your soul is healing your body. Self-care is healthy.

Your thoughts are your energy. Energy is life. It's time to level-up your thoughts and your energy. The process of divorce does damage to our self-esteem, our confidence, our feelings about ourselves and our thoughts. We can quickly think we are failures or bad people because our marriage failed. I ask you to do Louise's work and amp up your healing process by improving your self- confidence/self-esteem work now. It is not silly. It is healthy.

My next savior is Cheryl Richardson. Her books *Take Time for Your Life*, *Stand Up For Your Life* and *Life Makeover* gave me the courage and tools to quit my obligatory, draining job in 2002. This was the first step I needed to take to leave my marriage. Her work is brilliant and so well-written. Her work inspired me to create a life makeover group with a dear friend who was also taking time for her life. When I look back, it was the work of Anne, Louise and Cheryl that empowered me to take the first steps to heal my life back at the age of 37.

Two more women inspired me along the way. Suzanne Somers' work in the field of women's hormonal health. She has written many books. I suggest you read her latest as she is always writing a new improved, more up to date version of her work. She is a pioneer in the field of Functional/Integrative Medicine. I suggest you get baseline blood work and know where your hormones stand. It is the future of your health and longevity.

And lovely Kris Carr *Crazy Sexy Cancer and Crazy Sexy Kitchen* are my go-to knowledge books and recipes.
Kris is a Goddess and a bright light in the cancer and wellness world. Get to know her, study from her and begin your new chapter wiser and empowered.

Your new life begins with wellness.

What wellness looks like to you may be very different than what wellness looks like to me. Wellness: Healing work of yoga, chiropractic, bodywork, energy work, etc. Explore all these avenues and make a promise to yourself that you will never lie to yourself and you will never wear a mask. We are ready for our final Lesson Six.

I am not sure if we should smile or cry. See you on the other side.

Lesson Six
Celebrate Every Success

We shouldn't see a celebration as a party for the sake of a party. The definition of a celebration is the act, process of showing appreciation, gratitude and remembrance of something well done or achieved.

Let's start by celebrating the success of your completion of this life-changing course.
What are my lessons?
What have I learned about myself, my relationships, the process of divorce and the outcome I desire and deserve?

 **Here we go one more time. It's time to journal.**

Take some time to get quiet. Take some time to sit tall, take a few slow deep breaths and contemplate where you were when you began this course and where you are now.

- Who am I now?
- How am I different?
- Who do I cherish?
- Who cherishes me?
- What are my goals?
- How will I achieve them?
- What have I let go of?
- What do I need to prioritize?
- What am I most proud of?
- Who do I want to be in the future?
- How can I serve others?
- What are my gifts?

- What have I learned from this experience?
- How can I protect myself from making similar mistakes?
- What is my purpose in life?

Recognizing that change is a catalyst for growth, how do you measure each step?

Can you find an accountability partner? How can you continue to commit to your own self-awareness, growth, knowledge and strength? What skills do you now have that you didn't have before that can help you stay on track? After you've gone through the five stages of grief, what is the lesson?

Carry those lessons with you.
- I am stronger than I thought I was.
- I am worthy of so much more.
- I am not the wreck that others say I am.
- I am a good person who deserves to be unconditionally loved.
- I deserve to not be abused, lied to and taken for granted.
- I will not settle for less.
- I have the power to create the life I deserve and desire.
- I will forgive myself for all my mistakes.
- I will let go of trying to control others.
- I am in control of my thoughts, feelings, reactions and outcome.
- I am free of the past.
- I am deserving of a better life.
- I will have all the love, laughter and community I need.

Now it's time to reinvent yourself…what does that mean to you? Describe the new you. Describe your new life.

- Tell me! Write me an email and share with me the new you and your new life.
- Shout it out. Embrace it. Share the new you with the world.

- The world needs more women like you who are willing to do the hard work.
- The world needs more women like you who are willing to make the world a better place.
- The world needs more women like you who are willing to take off the mask, be real, honest, raw and authentic and be an example of what living their best life ever means.

Even if others don't approve or reject you or judge you or disregard you, condemn you, ignore you, unfriend you, disown you, sue you, leave you, block you and yes…hate you.

They were not meant to be in your life to begin with. Mistakes were made. Forgiveness is healing. You are free. It may feel like you're not making progress if you are not celebrating the tiny successes, even the smallest mindset shift is a success. I encourage you to reach out to me to continue this journey we started together.

How do you still need guidance? How can I help you create the life you desire and deserve? The way forward is clear.

Coaching will encourage you to: Never stop learning, never stop growing, never stop loving.

- Your future is yours to create and only you can do that.
- But it's never easy to do alone.
- We all need support and guidance along the way.
- I would never have survived my journey without expert help and coaching along the way.
- It's easy to lose our way somewhere along the journey.
- Don't question how you found me…just know there is a reason. I am so proud of you. You did it!!!

NOTES

REVIEW
NO MISTAKES ...ONLY LESSONS.

Let's recap a few highlights.

Have you decided if changing your name is worth it?
It took me two years to start the process. Give it a bit of time before you rush into it.

The beginning of taking control of your new life is on paper.
Writing a goal or vision down gains strength and energy when you write it down.
A goal is birthed when you express it out loud and write it down on paper.

 **Name three accountable goals that are very important to you that you can achieve in 6-18 months.**

Know your relationship patterns, so you don't make a habit of repeating them.

How much of a priority is your healing?

How can you practice GRACE as you start your day every day?

How will you celebrate each small victory you achieve?

You need to reward yourself. Chapter Eight is about you prioritizing yourself and creating a foundation for you to build your new life. Take these skills and use them. They will guide you into your new life.

Congratulations– you've completed all 8 modules of the
Better Divorce Academy course.
This journey is without a doubt one of the most challenging
processes you can ever embark on.

Divorce is a death. Divorce is an ending.

Divorce feels like a failure but ends up being a new life that is created by the gift of personal courage, patience, persistence and self-love.

Divorce survival is about thriving in the chaos and coming out the other side: newer, brighter, clearer and more beautiful.

Stepping into your power, your strength and your ability to reinvent yourself into a better version of yourself.

If you need additional support, keep in mind all the additional tools you have to work with me.

Schedule your free 45-minute consultation with me via **Betterdivorceacademy.com,** where we can discuss what you need and how I can help.

CONTINUING YOUR JOURNEY WITH ME

Schedule your private 45-minute consultation with me via www.betterdivorceacademy.com where the two of us can confidentially discuss what you need and how I can best serve you and your goals.

1. Luxury Exclusive Stand In The Fire With You Certified Divorce Coaching

2. Private 1:1 Certified Divorce Coach/Trauma Informed Certified Divorce Specialist

3. Sacred Space Inner Circle Closed Private Group Online Course, Coaching and Resources

4. Best Life Ever Virtual and Elite \Private Planning and Recovery Retreats

5. The Thriving In Chaos Project Podcast

6. Better Career Project Business and Book Creation Launch

7. Elite Confidential Mediation Services

8. Expert High Touch Master Mediation Divorce Team Creation and Resolution

9. No Matter What Inspirational Card Deck

10. Better Divorce Blueprint: The Book, The Journal and Eight Module Online Course

PAULETTE RIGO

Paulette Rigo is a Credentialed Mediator, Certified Divorce Coach, Trauma Informed Recovery Coach, Career Transition Specialist, E-RYT500, author of Better Divorce Blueprint the online course, book, planner and No Matter What card deck, Host of The Thriving in Chaos Project Podcast, Creator of Best Life Ever Retreats and founder of Better Divorce Academy, her commitment to creating an optimal divorce experience is her life's work.

It's Paulette's personal experience, high level guidance, resources and expertise that makes her continually strive to create a better way to divorce from the early stage of contemplation to the necessary final steps of healing using practical tools, inspiration and a proven road map for living out your dreams and desire to become who you were meant to be.

THANK YOU FROM MY HEART TO YOURS.

I thank you for taking this journey with me. I deeply thank Sonia Queralt, Casey Shevin and Tali Koss for sharing their legal brilliance and the power of Divorceify with me.

It is my desire that you feel a deeper sense of clarity, preparation and empowerment to thrive throughout the process of divorce. Know you are not alone. I am here to help guide and support you each step of the way.

Remember that private one-on-one coaching is always helpful. Just as each marriage is unique, each divorce is too.

If you found this book (and online course) useful, please do take the time to leave a review on Amazon. This small step will help me reach and help more people just like you.

With gratitude and love,

Paulette G. Rigo

Paulette Rigo

BIBLIOGRAPHY AND REFERENCES

On Death and Dying by Elizabeth Kubler-Ross

David Kessler https://grief.com/

Carrie Cole from the Gottman Institute: https://www.gottman.com/

Signs of an uphappy marriage: https://news.yahoo.com/10-signs-youre-unhappy-marriage-172127468.html

KOLBE index: https://www.kolbe.com/

Rosalind Sedacca. She is the founder of the Child-Centered Divorce Network
How Do I Tell the Kids about the Divorce? by Rosalind Sedacca

Bronnie Ware: The Top Five Regrets of the Dying

Parent Education Programs
https://www.mwi.org/look-forward-to-your-parent-education-program/
Comparing 36 western countries in 2005/06, Thoroddur Bjarnason studied the proportion of 11-15-year-old children living in different child custody arrangements

GRACE Trails from my dear friend, mentor and author Anne Jolles

5 Reasons Why Divorce May be Good for You!. https://www.family-lawrights.net/blog/5-reasons-why-divorce-may-be-good-for-you/

The 5 Stages of Grief & Loss - Psych Central. https://psychcentral.com/lib/the-5-stages-of-loss-and-grief/

17 Signs You're In an Unhappy Marriage - MSN. https://www.msn.com/en-us/lifestyle/love-sex/17-signs-youre-in-an-unhappy-marriage/ar-BBNQ6xP

5 Essential Secrets To Emotional Well-Being | Eva Gregory. https://evagregory.com/5-essential-secrets-to-emotional-well-being/

Conscious Dating – Red Flags Checklist. http://www.getrcimedia.com/members/external/datingredflags.pdf

Best way for parents to break the divorce news to your kids https://www.childcentereddivorce.com/coaching-programs/kids/

Regrets of the Dying - Bronnie Ware. https://bronnieware.com/regrets-of-the-dying/
Getting Down to Basics with Meditation - recoveryouresteem. https://recoveryouresteem.com/getting-down-to-basics-with-meditation/

Marital Property Definition - Investopedia. https://www.investopedia.com/terms/m/maritalproperty.asp

10 Biggest Divorce Mediation Benefits. https://www.equitablemediation.com/blog/10-biggest-divorce-mediation-benefits
Child Custody Attorney Salt Lake City Utah | John Vitela. https://whisente11.wordpress.com/2020/06/12/child-custody-attorney-salt-lake-city-utah/

50/50 Custody & Visitation Schedules: 6 Most Common Examples. https://www.custodyxchange.com/examples/schedules/50-50/

Parental Alienation - Definition, Examples, Cases, Processes. https://legaldictionary.net/parental-alienation/

Made in the USA
Columbia, SC
05 July 2023

20021232R00167